David Young

Computer Programming in BASIC

Lionel Carter is a qualified Chartered Mechanical Engineer. He is Principal Lecturer in Management Science at Slough College of Higher Education and a visiting lecturer at Brunel University. Previously he was an operational research consultant in industry. He has acted as an adviser to the EITB in developing an investment appraisal training programme.

Dr Eva Huzan is Head of the Computing Division at Slough College of Higher Education. Previously she worked as a physicist and computing lecturer in industry. She has carried out research in computing and physics at the London School of Economics and Political Science, and Queen Mary College, University of London.

The authors have collaborated before in writing *A Practical Approach to Computer Simulation in Business* (1973) and *The Pocket Calculator*, Teach Yourself Books (1979). They also have had several articles published in professional journals.

TEACH YOURSELF BOOKS

Computer Programming in BASIC

L. R. Carter M.Tech., C.Eng.,
M.I.Mech.E., M.B.C.S., F.O.R.
E. Huzan B.Sc., Ph.D., F.B.C.S.

TEACH YOURSELF BOOKS
Hodder and Stoughton

First Printed 1981
Second impression 1981

Published in the USA by David Mckay & Co. Inc., 750 Third
Avenue, New York, NY 10017, USA.

British Library C.I.P.

Carter, L R
  Computer programming in Basic. – (Teach
  yourself books).
  1. Basic (Computer program language)
  I. Title   II. Series
  001.6′424   QA76.73.B3

  ISBN 0–340–24882–3

Printed and bound in Great Britain for Hodder and Stoughton
paperbacks, a division of Hodder and Stoughton Ltd, Mill Road,
Dunton Green, Sevenoaks, Kent, (Editorial Office: 47 Bedford
Square, London, WC1 3DP) by Richard Clay (The Chaucer
Press), Ltd., Bungay, Suffolk

Contents

List of Figures

List of Tables

Introduction

This book is designed to enable you to learn to program a computer in easy stages and in a methodical way, using the BASIC programming language. You will find that most computers accept programs written in this language.

A computer, compared with a non-programmable calculator, is able to store in its memory the complete set of instructions needed to solve a particular problem. Available instructions include those to read data, to perform calculations and compare values, and to output results. The computer will work through the programmed instructions automatically once the run has been initiated. Chapter 1 explains how computers perform these functions and the typical equipment that comprises a computer system.

The computer that you may have access to will have a set of system commands which you will need to learn before you can enter BASIC programs into it and run the programs with data. These commands vary according to the system you are using. For example, if you use a terminal linked to a large computer you may need to log in and use a password. Alternatively, you may submit your BASIC programs and data on punched cards or paper tape for batch processing and have the output returned to you at a later stage. If you are using a microcomputer, then this may be available to you in the classroom, laboratory, office or home.

Chapter 6 discusses some of the typical commands that you may encounter when using any of these systems, and is intended to be used for reference purposes to give an understanding of the different types of system commands. However, you will need to become familiar with the few essential commands required for running BASIC on *your system* when you begin to study the language in Chapter 2. When you have completed Chapter 2, you should be able to write and run some very simple BASIC programs. Test yourself with the list of questions given at the end of Chapter 2 before you proceed.

Arithmetic operations are covered in Chapter 3, and, as in subsequent chapters, examples are given within the text together with problems for you to program and run on your computer. You can compare your programs with those listed in Appendix A; answers to the problems, where these are not given in the text, will be found in Appendix B.

For problems other than very simple ones you must plan and design your programs in such a way that you ensure that all requirements are met and the likelihood of errors is minimised. Chapter 4 suggests an approach to help you develop programs efficiently. The types of error that can occur, their detection and correction are discussed and illustrated in Chapter 5 together with a method for testing your programs thoroughly.

Once a program is fully tested and operational it may be used repeatedly with different data by the programmer and other users. Amendments may need to be made later in response to changed circumstances. For a program to be used effectively and amended easily, it is essential to have comprehensive documentation for it. Typical information that should be included in your documentation is given in the final section of Chapter 5.

Having learnt the essential features of programming, you will need additional BASIC statements to enable you to program 'real' problems. Chapters 7, 8, 9 and 10 deal with branching, functions, arrays and subroutines, respectively. The routines developed may be used in a variety of programs and this is further illustrated in Chapter 12.

BASIC is the acronym for Beginners All-purpose Symbolic Instruction Code, and was designed and used originally for teaching programming. Since then many extensions have been made to it. In particular, BASIC may now be used for the creation and processing of data files on secondary storage devices. The BASIC statements used for these procedures are not standard, however Chapter 11 illustrates the essential requirements associated with file processing.

The examples and problems in Chapters 7–11 illustrate the use of BASIC programs in different fields of application. Chapter 12 illustrates particular features of programming, such as iterative procedures, interactive running, tabulation of results and the use of previously developed routines, by means of applications in the fields of mathematics, statistics, science, engineering and management.

1 Introduction to Computers and Programming

1.1 Basic functions and units of a computer

An essential function of a computer is the ability to store the set of instructions required to process a particular task. This set of instructions (the *program*), which is prepared by a programmer, has to be held in the computer's store (its main *memory*) while the instructions are followed.

Each computer has a fixed instruction set which it can execute. A *control unit* selects the instructions, one at a time, from the memory, decodes or interprets them and causes the computer to carry out the instruction. If the instruction requires an arithmetic operation to be performed then the control unit transfers the necessary data between the memory and the *arithmetic and logic unit*.

The main memory, arithmetic and logic unit, and control unit comprise the central part of the computer, and together are known as the *central processor*.

Input and *output* peripheral devices, linked to the central processor, are used to insert programs and data into the computer's memory and to output results from there. Typical input devices read and decode patterns of punched holes on cards or paper tape, or sense marks optically or magnetically, and transmit this information electronically to the central processor. Alternatively, the information can be keyed in directly from a keyboard (similar to that of a typewriter). Results may be displayed on a television screen or visual display unit, or, if a 'hard' copy is required, printers are available which print either one character or a complete line at a time across a page. Graph plotters may also be used as output peripherals.

Programs may be stored magnetically on *backing* or *secondary storage* devices, and these can then be read back into the computer's memory when required. On large (mainframe) computers, magnetic discs and tape are used for this purpose, while on the smaller microcomputers the equivalent devices are floppy discs and cassettes which hold less information and transfer it much more slowly. Other forms of secondary storage, such as magnetic bubble memories, are also available.

Secondary storage devices are also used to hold files of data records. These are transferred to and from the computer's memory under program control for file processing applications.

Figure 1.1 shows the basic units of a computer, the flow of data and control links.

1.2 How information is held

A computer is largely made up of a number of two-state devices. The 'off' state of the device may be considered to represent a 0 and the 'on' state a 1. A numbering system comprising only 0s and 1s is called a *binary system*. Different patterns of these binary digits (or *bits*) may be used to represent a character set and ranges of numbers.

Standard codes have been established by different organisations. The American Standard Code for Information Interchange (ASCII) has been widely adopted, and a table showing the binary representations for a 64 character set is shown in Appendix C. This is the character set that is most commonly available. Extensions to the ASCII 64 character set allow the representation of additional characters such as lower case alphabet characters (a, b, c etc.).

Numbers are represented in the computer's memory as a combination of bits. The number of bits available to repre-

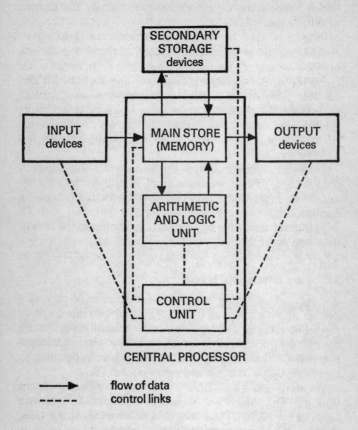

Figure 1.1 Basic units of a computer

sent a number varies with the computer used. When using BASIC, most systems will work in floating point arithmetic, in which numbers are held as a *mantissa* and an *exponent*. For example, $6 \times 10^3 = 6000$, has a mantissa of 6 and an exponent of 3.

From the BASIC user's point of view, the two factors that should be established are the precision of the decimal number (which is defined by the number of bits used to hold the mantissa), and the range of numbers that can be held in the computer (which is defined by the number of bits used to hold the exponent).

Codes for paper tape and cards are not standard. This means that a BASIC program or data punched for one system may not run on a different computer, although the actual programming instructions are acceptable to both. This non-compatibility of codes also applies to other peripheral media. A thorough understanding of the standards and ranges of numbers for the system(s) you are using, therefore, is essential.

1.3 Programming a computer

Each family of processors has its own instruction set which is likely to differ from that of other processors. This means that a particular processor is only capable of understanding its own set of instructions in *binary code*.

The computer's memory can be considered as consisting of a number of cells capable of storing binary patterns representing program instructions or data. Each of these cells is uniquely numbered so that reference can be made to particular memory cells, either to select a program instruction or data, or to write data into a certain memory cell.

As an example of how programs are written in a computer's own code (machine code), it will be assumed that two numbers are held in memory cells 5 and 6, that these are to be added together, and the result stored in memory cell 8. The addition will be performed in a storage location called the *accumulator*, so the first instruction needs to load one of the numbers into the accumulator. The second instruction adds the other number to the number in the accumulator, which will then contain the sum of the two numbers. The third instruction stores the contents of the accumulator in the required memory cell.

The binary codes for these instructions for a typical processor are shown in Table 1.1.

	Instruction	Machine code	
1	Load number held in memory cell 5 into accumulator	10100101	0101
2	Add number held in memory cell 6 to number in accumulator	01100101	0110
3	Store number held in accumulator in memory cell 8	10000101	1000

Table 1.1   Machine code instructions

In one program run, memory cells 5 and 6 could have been set to 700 and 250, respectively. After the three instructions in Table 1.1 have been obeyed, cells 5 and 6 would still contain 700 and 250 and cell 8 would now contain 700 + 250 i.e. 950. The same program could be run again with different data in cells 5 and 6 (say 43 and 12), which would result in cell 8 having its previous value of 950 replaced by the new value of 55.

1.4   Programming languages

As you have seen, programming in the computer's own machine code requires that the instructions and data are given to it in binary. Writing down and keying in a series of 1s and 0s is time-consuming and prone to error. An alternative way of expressing the instructions is to use *mnemonic codes.* For example, the command to load a number from a memory cell could be written as LDA instead of, say, 10100101. Also the memory cells could be given symbolic names instead of referring to them by their actual numeric (binary) addresses.

This type of programming language is used when it is necessary to have close control over the functions of the computer. Languages which use such mnemonic codes are known as *assembly languages*. Each assembly language instruction usually corresponds to an equivalent machine code instruction. The translation of the assembly language program into machine code is carried out by a machine code program called an *assembler*.

High-level languages have been devised which allow several machine code instructions to be expressed in one statement. BASIC is such a programming language as shown in the example below:

$$\text{LET C} = \text{A} + \text{B}$$

is a BASIC statement which causes the two numbers, held in memory cells called A and B, to be added together and the sum stored in memory cell C. This is the same problem which previously required three machine code or assembly language instructions.

However, neither assembly language nor BASIC programs can be understood directly by the computer. BASIC programs need to be translated into machine code using a *compiler* or *interpreter*.

1.5 Compilers and interpreters

If a BASIC program is compiled, the compiler (which is a machine code program) translates each statement in the BASIC program (the *source program*) into machine code, adds additional library routines if required, and produces an *object program* which is the machine code equivalent of the original BASIC source program. The object program may then be run with data as a normal machine code program.

One of the advantages of compiling BASIC programs is that the translation process has only to be carried out once (if there are no errors), since a compiled version (the object program) may be run whenever that program is required to process data.

However, most BASIC systems use interpretive machine code routines to translate the BASIC statements. The BASIC interpreter scans each statement after it has been input and searches for the keyword in that statement, which it interprets as a command. The execution of the BASIC instructions is carried out by executing the commands by machine code routines. A machine code object program is *not* produced, so that the BASIC program has to be interpreted each time it is used.

The writing of BASIC programs is the same whether they are to be interpreted or compiled.

2 Simple Input and Output Statements

2.1 READ, DATA, INPUT and PRINT statements

This chapter explains how you may enter information into the computer (*input*), and how the computer may be programmed to supply information, for example on a printer or video screen (*output*).

Each BASIC instruction (or statement) consists of a command to the computer to carry out a certain action, and a combination of variables, constants, separators (e.g. a comma) and operators (e.g. +) on which the action is to be performed. For example:

10 READ A,B,C

tells the computer to read three numbers (numeric constants) from the DATA statement (see line 20 below) and store them in three cells in the computer memory identified by the names A, B and C. A, B and C are called *variables* and refer to unique numeric addresses, as explained in Chapter 1 p. 9. When A, B or C are referenced again in the *same* program, the computer will obtain the current contents of these cells. In a *different* program, A, B and C may refer to cells with different actual numeric addresses but unique for *that* program. Single memory cells are referenced in BASIC programs by single letters of the alphabet, A–Z, followed optionally by a single number, 0–9.

The 10 before READ in the statement above is the *line number*. Line numbers enable you to change particular lines in your program by retyping the line. Gaps may be left in the sequence of line numbers for subsequent insertion of additional instructions. Three further instructions com-

plete the program to read and output (PRINT) three
numbers:

20 DATA 25,11,30
30 PRINT A,B,C
40 END

The END statement tells the computer that this is the end
of the BASIC program, so that the computer run (i.e. the
processing of the program instructions) is stopped.

Note that the following three statements have the same
effect as the above READ statement. That is, after these
three instructions have been executed with the DATA statement shown in line 20, A, B and C will contain 25, 11 and
30 respectively.

10 READ A
11 READ B
12 READ C

The way you enter BASIC programs into the computer
depends on the computer system you are using. Chapter 6
discusses different system commands that may be available
for use with your computer. Find out which system commands you need to enter a BASIC program and to run it,
and then practise with this program.

Note in particular how the contents of A, B and C (i.e. 25,
11 and 30) are output and the number of spaces between the
numbers. Change the program so that the PRINT statement
is as follows:

30 PRINT A;B;C

and note the spacing between the numbers when a semicolon
is used to separate the variables in a PRINT statement
instead of a comma.

To change the data, you will need to alter the numbers in
the DATA statement. Alternatively, you may use an
INPUT statement instead of READ and DATA statements.

Replace the READ and DATA statements in the program by the following statement:

10 INPUT A,B,C

You will need to find out how to delete line 20, which is no longer required. When this program is run interactively from a computer terminal or on a microcomputer, the computer will output a question-mark (?), or some other character depending on the system used, to indicate that data should be input from the keyboard or some other device. If your BASIC programs are being run in batch mode, you will need to supply the data at the end of your program so that it is read after the END statement.

A heading may be output at the beginning of the output from the computer by putting it in double quotation marks in a PRINT statement as in the following example:

28 PRINT "A", "B", "C"
30 PRINT A,B,C

(*Note*: In computer codes the *same* character is used for open and closed double quotation marks.)

An alternative method of identifying the three numbers is to output A = followed by the number. Experiment with the following statement to obtain the spacing you require (delete line 28):

30 PRINT "A =";A, "B =";B, "C =";C

The information in the double quotes is output as given in line 30, while A, B and C which are *not* in quotes refer to memory cells. If A, B and C contain 25, 11 and 30 respectively, line 30 will output:

A = 25   B = 11   C = 30

The spacing will depend on how your computer system interprets a comma and a semicolon in a PRINT statement.

You may put extra spaces (∇ indicates a space) between the quotation marks. For example, substituting,

$$\text{"}\nabla\nabla\nabla\nabla\nabla A\nabla =\text{"}$$

in statement 30 above would result in A being output with five spaces before it and one space before the equals sign.

The TAB function may be used to output information in particular column positions on your video screen or printed page, as illustrated in the following example:

```
30 PRINT TAB(5);"A =";A;
                TAB(15);"B =";B;TAB(25);"C =";C
```

For most systems, this will cause A = to be output in positions 6, 7 and 8, followed by the contents of cell A, then B = in positions 16, 17 and 18, followed by the contents of cell B, then C = in positions 26, 27 and 28 followed by the contents of cell C. Some systems use the value in the TAB brackets as the print position. You should test this for your system.

The TAB function will be discussed further in subsequent chapters.

2.2 String variables

For many problems it is necessary to input, store and output variable information which consists of a mixture of letters, numbers and special characters, including spaces. Such a series of symbols is called a *string*. Strings may be stored in *string variables*. These must be given a name consisting of one of the alphabetic letters A–Z, followed by a dollar sign $, that is, A$, B$, C$, ..., Z$. You may need to reserve storage space in the memory, for each of the string variables that you use in your program, by means of a DIM statement. For example, the statement:

$$5 \text{ DIM D\$ (7), N\$ (19)}$$

will reserve storage in the memory for a maximum of eight characters for D$ and twenty characters for N$. Only some BASIC systems have this requirement, so check if this is the case for your computer system. Section 9.4 in Chapter 9 describes the more usual use of DIM, for defining storage for arrays.

The constant information given in double quotes previously is termed *a string constant*.

String variables are essential for reading in and manipulating files of information, particularly for business applications. Just a few examples of the use of string variables are given here to give you some initial practice.

Once a program has been written and proved correct, it may be used over and over again with different data, on different occasions and by different people. It is useful, therefore, to output the date the program has been run, and perhaps by whom. Two string variables may be used to input this information and to cause it to be output.

Change and insert statements in the program to output three numbers as follows:

```
10 INPUT A,B,C,D$,N$
26 PRINT
27 PRINT "DATE RUN";D$;TAB(25);N$
28 PRINT
```

When this amended program is run, in reply to ? you will need to input three numbers separated by commas (for A, B and C), followed by the date and your name. The requirements for inputting strings may vary from system to system. Generally, the string constant in a DATA statement or in response to an INPUT statement needs to be in double quotes if the string contains a comma, semicolon or space, or if the first character of the string is a numeric digit, decimal point, $+$ or $-$ sign. For example, data for the above program could be:

? 25,11,30,"26/11/80", J.SMITH

Try running this program with different data, different dates and your name. Notice that the PRINT statements at lines 26 and 28 output blank lines.

2.3   Obtaining the required print layout

It is important to design suitable output so that this can be output in different formats for different purposes. Various ways of using name and address information will be used to illustrate this. The program given in Table 2.1 inputs a title (MR, MRS, MISS etc.), a name and an address, so that this is stored in memory cells referenced by string variables, and outputs a letter heading, notebook label and envelope labels.

The six INPUT statements shown in Table 2.1 will cause the computer to request six lines of data to be input. When working interactively, each line of data is entered in response to the ? output by the computer as shown in Table 2.2. Notice that you must have exactly six lines of data; if necessary, enter a space (blank) for the last two lines to complete the data.

Enter and run the program on your computer. Also find out how to save the program, so that you can access it later on for amendment. For example, the program statements may be stored on disc, magnetic tape or cassettes, which may be used subsequently to read the BASIC program back into the computer memory so that statements may be changed if required before the program is run.

The REM (remarks) statements at lines 70, 150 and 290, in Table 2.1, are only listed with the program to explain the program's actions. It is assumed that a minimum width of forty characters is available on your video screen or on the computer printout. Letter headings are normally printed in the top right-hand corner of the page, and in this case the four line address is output starting at position twenty (or nineteen depending on the TAB implementation). If more

```
10  INPUT T$
20  INPUT N$
30  INPUT A$
40  INPUT B$
50  INPUT C$
60  INPUT D$
70  REM PRINT LETTER HEADING
80  PRINT TAB(19) ;A$
90  PRINT TAB(19) ;B$
100  PRINT TAB(19) ;C$
110  PRINT TAB(19) ;D$
120  PRINT
130  PRINT
140  PRINT
150  REM PRINT NOTEBOOK LABEL
160  PRINT
170  PRINT
180  PRINT
190  PRINT TAB(7) ;"*********************"
200  PRINT
210  PRINT
220  PRINT TAB(9) ;N$
230  PRINT
240  PRINT
250  PRINT TAB(7) ;"*********************"
260  PRINT
270  PRINT
280  PRINT
290  REM PRINT ENVELOPE LABELS
300  PRINT
310  PRINT
320  PRINT
330  PRINT T$;" ";N$;TAB(19) ;T$;" ";N$
340  PRINT A$;TAB(19) ;A$
350  PRINT B$;TAB(19) ;B$
360  PRINT C$;TAB(19) ;C$
370  PRINT D$;TAB(19) ;D$
380  END
```

Table 2.1 Name and address program

characters are available across the screen or page, then the spacing in the PRINT statements may be altered to allow for this. You can make this spacing variable by replacing the number 19, in brackets after TAB in lines 80–110, by a

```
? "MR"
? "J. SMITH"
? "1 THE AVENUE"
? "LONDON W8"
? " "
? " "
```

Table 2.2   Data for program

variable, say I; a value for I may then be entered at run time in response to an additional instruction:

75 INPUT I

The notebook label will contain just the name of the owner in between two lines of asterisks. However, at this stage you will not be able to centralise the name, according to its length, for names of varying length. This will be dealt with in Chapter 7 as an example of the use of test instructions.

The envelope labels are printed two side by side. The spacing can be controlled by TAB (I) as before, using the same value for I, or a different value may be entered by means of another INPUT instruction.

If you have worked through this chapter step by step, you should be able to answer all the following questions. Test yourself referring to the appropriate sections in this chapter if necessary; you may also need to consult your computer system manual and output from your computer.

2.4 Questions

1 Explain what a variable is in BASIC.
2 Which system command did you use before entering your BASIC program?
3 Which system command did you use to run your BASIC program?
4 How did you change an instruction in your BASIC program?
5 How did you delete an instruction in your BASIC program?
6 How did you insert an instruction in your BASIC program?
7 If the computer outputs a single question mark (?) during the running of a program, what does this indicate?
8 In which positions are numbers output on your computer when there are *commas* between the variables in a PRINT statement?
9 In which positions are numbers output on your computer when there are *semicolons* between the variables in a PRINT statement?
10 How are string constants represented in BASIC?
11 What are string variables and how may they be used?
12 What is the purpose of the TAB function? Give an example.
13 What is the purpose of the REM statement?

3 Arithmetic Operations

3.1 Constants and variables

The computer may be programmed to perform a variety of calculations by means of arithmetic assignment statements in which the result of the calculation is assigned to a memory cell. For example:

$$50 \text{ LET } S = X + Y$$

causes the computer to add the contents of memory cell X to that of memory cell Y and puts the result in a memory cell called S. X and Y will have had values assigned to them previously, either by an INPUT or READ + DATA statements or by another LET statement. The contents of cells X and Y are unchanged by the action of the LET statement. For example, Table 3.1 shows the contents of X, Y and S

Cell	Before	After
X	123	123
Y	56	56
S	?	179

Table 3.1   Contents of X, Y and S

before and after execution of the above LET statement, in a program which contains the following statements in addition to line 50 above:

> 30 READ X,Y
> 40 DATA 123,56

Note the original, unknown, contents of S has been over-written by the new value 179, the sum of 123 and 56.

The variables on the right-hand side of the equals sign in a LET statement may be operated on by a number of different arithmetic operators, and may be mixed with constant values (constants). For example:

$$51 \text{ LET I} = \text{I} - 1$$

subtracts 1 from the current value of I, so that after the LET statement has been obeyed I has a value one less than its previous value.

The *variable names* that may be used in a BASIC program to store *numbers* in memory cells must consist only of the letters A–Z, and any of these single letters followed by the number 0–9. That is:

A,B,C, . . ., Z
A0,A1,A2, . . ., A9
.
.
.
Z0,Z1,Z2, . . ., Z9

Thus there are a total of 286 possible names in standard BASIC. On some extended BASIC systems more than one alphabetic letter is allowed to give a larger number of names that may be used.

The *numeric constants* that may be used are:

a) whole numbers (*integers*) which do not contain a decimal point, for example, $-45,360$ (or $+360$);

b) numbers containing a decimal point, for example, 8.123, -97.5;

c) numbers in exponential format, for example, 12.3E4, which represents $12.3 \times 10^4 = 123000$ (4 is called the exponent). The exponent may also be negative, for example, $12.3E - 4$, which is $12.3 \times 10^{-4} = 0.00123$.

Note that numbers are made *negative* by putting a minus sign $(-)$ in front of them; A plus sign $(+)$, or *no* sign, indicates the number is *positive*.

Any number that is used in the program, either as a constant or as the contents of a variable, must lie within the range of the computer that you are using. Find out the largest and smallest numbers that can be used on your computer, and make sure that the data you input, use in calculations and try to store, are all within the range of your computer.

3.2 Arithmetic operators

The symbols on the right-hand side of the equals sign in a LET statement may consist of variable names, constants and arithmetic operators; this combination of symbols is called an *arithmetic expression*. The *arithmetic operators* indicate which arithmetic operation is to be carried out on the numbers in the arithmetic expression.

Arithmetic operators	*Meaning*
+	add
−	subtract
*	multiply
/	divide
↑	raise to a power (exponentiation)

3.3 Hierarchy of operations

It is possible to use brackets in an arithmetic expression to make it meaningful. The contents of the brackets are evaluated first starting with the innermost pair of brackets and working outwards. For example, to evaluate

$$\frac{5+9}{4+3}$$

the top line (*numerator*) needs to be added first, then the bottom line (*denominator*) needs to be added, and finally the

numerator is divided by the denominator. Brackets are used
to ensure this order of evaluation.

A program to illustrate the order of evaluation is given
in Table 3.2; the larger gap in the sequence of line numbers

```
30 READ B,C,D,E
40 DATA 5,9,4,3
50 LET A = (B + C)/(D + E)
70 PRINT B,C,D,E,A
80 END
```

Table 3.2 Program to illustrate order of evaluation

between the LET and PRINT statements will allow the
insertion of additional statements later. Table 3.3 shows the
contents of the memory cells before and after the LET
statement in line 50 has been obeyed.

Cell	B	C	D	E	A
Before	5	9	4	3	?
After	5	9	4	3	2

Table 3.3 Contents of B, C, D, E and A

Run this program on your computer and then amend the
LET statement as follows (i.e. remove the brackets).

$$50 \text{ LET } A = B + C/D + E$$

A will now be 10.25 (i.e. $\frac{9}{4} + 5 + 3$). This is because the

computer evaluates the arithmetic expression in a certain
order if there are no brackets, depending on the arithmetic
operators in the expression.

If there are no brackets, then the computer will perform
the exponentiations first (if there are any), followed by
multiplication and division of equal hierarchy, but in the
order left to right, lastly addition and subtraction of equal
hierarchy. Within brackets the same order of evaluation is

carried out, innermost brackets being calculated first as previously stated.

Looking again at the last statement at line 50, you will see that the division, C/D, has been carried out first as it is of higher hierarchy than addition. This gives a completely different result from that calculated in the previous LET statement in Table 3.2 where brackets were used.

3.4 Arithmetic expressions and statements

Insert all the LET and PRINT statements shown in Table 3.4 into your program and run it. Output all the results

```
50  LET A = (B + C)/(D + E)
51  LET G = C/E — B*D
52  LET H = C/(E — B)*D
53  LET J = G — H/E+E↑2
61  LET S = C*D — B↑A
62  LET T = (C*D — B)↑A
63  LET U = (E*(C — B)↑(D/A))
70  PRINT
71  PRINT
72  PRINT "B =";B;"C =";C;"D =";D;"E =";E
73  PRINT
74  PRINT
75  PRINT "A =";A;"G =";G;"H =";H;"J =";J
76  PRINT
77  PRINT
78  PRINT "S =";S;"T =";T;"U =";U
```

Table 3.4 LET statements

(A,G,H,J,S,T,U) together with the variable names as identification. The data read and the final results are shown in Table 3.5.

$$B = 5 \quad C = 9 \quad D = 4 \quad E = 3$$
$$A = 2 \quad G = -17 \quad H = -18 \quad J = -2$$
$$S = 11 \quad T = 961 \quad U = 48$$

Table 3.5 Data read and final results

Notes

1　Line 51 could be replaced by

　　51 LET G = (C/E) — (B∗D)

　　to give the same result, although the brackets are unnecessary in this case.

2　The brackets in line 52 are essential to give the correct answer, as can be seen by comparing the results of line 52 with that of line 51.

3　In line 53, H is used in the expression because a value was assigned to it in line 52. Instead of E↑2, you can use E∗E which is a quicker operation on most computers. Amend line 53 to

　　53 LET J = G — H/E+E∗E

　　and check that you get the same result for J.

4　In line 61, B↑A (i.e. 5^2) is evaluated first, then C∗D (i.e. 9×4) before the subtraction (i.e. $36 - 25$) is carried out. However, in line 62 the contents of the brackets are evaluated first (i.e. 21) before this is squared by A.

5　There are three pairs of brackets in line 63. The innermost pair is evaluated first from the left, that is, C — B (equals 4), then D/A is evaluated (equals 2). The exponentiation is carried out next to give 4^2, and finally this is multiplied by E (i.e. 3).

As a further exercise, change the arithmetic expressions in lines 51–63 in Table 3.4 to those given in Table 3.6. Check

```
51  LET G = C/(E — B)*D
52  LET H = C/(E — B*D)
53  LET J = ((G — H)/E + E)↑2
61  LET S = C*(D — B)↑A
62  LET T = C*(D — B↑A)
63  LET U = E*C — B↑D/A
```

Table 3.6   Changes to arithmetic expressions

your results with those given in Table 3.7. Your computer may have the facility for changing individual characters in a line; use this facility, if possible, instead of typing whole lines again.

$$B = 5 \quad C = 9 \quad D = 4 \quad E = 3$$
$$A = 2 \quad G = -18 \quad H = -.529412 \quad J = 7.97232$$
$$S = 9 \quad T = -189 \quad U = -285.5$$

Table 3.7   Results of arithmetic operations

3.5   Problems

You are now ready to attempt some simple problems. For more complicated problems, it is advisable to express the logic in the form of a *flowchart* before coding it in BASIC, as explained in Chapter 4.

In your programs, use constants instead of variables for values that are not going to change during the execution of the program or from one run of the program to the next. Variable names should be meaningful: for example, use M for minutes.

Write programs and run them on your computer for each of the following problems. If you get errors, reading Chapters 5 and 6 will help you to correct them. Compare your programs with those given in Tables A1, A2 and A3 in Appendix A; substituting actual values in place of the variables will help you understand the action of each instruction. The output from each program for the data given is shown in Tables 3.8, 3.9 and 3.10. You should experiment with a variety of PRINT statements to give different outputs, e.g. underline answer with hyphens or asterisks, line up values.

Problem 1 – Hours and minutes

Starting with a variable time in hours (T1) and minutes (T2), for example 9.20 a.m., add on a variable number of minutes (M), for example 45 minutes, and print out the starting time, the number of minutes added and the new time, suitably identified.

After you have added T2 and M and divided by 60, you will need to add the integral part of the result (i.e. whole number of hours) to T1. If the result is in N2, say, then INT(N2) gives the integral part of N2. This can be added to T1 in a LET statement as follows:

$$40 \text{ LET } N1 = T1 + INT(N2)$$

The use of the INT function is explained further in Chapter 8.

```
STARTING TIME = 9 HOURS 20 MINUTES
NUMBER OF MINUTES ADDED = 45

NEW TIME = 10 HOURS 5 MINUTES
*************************************
```

Table 3.8 Output from 'Hours and minutes' program

Problem 2 – Number of £s required

On your proposed visit to the USA, you will need 26 dollars a night for accommodation and 43 dollars a day for food, travelling and incidental expenses. You intend to stay five nights and wish to take sufficient dollars to have 100 dollars to buy presents. How many pounds sterling will you need to exchange if the exchange rate is 2.05 dollars to the £? (Your program should be flexible enough to cope with changes in expenses, the length of stay and the exchange rate for subsequent visits.)

```
LENGTH OF STAY (NIGHTS)      : 5
ACCOMMODATION (PER NIGHT) $: 26
EXPENSES (MEALS ETC.)        $: 43
ALLOWANCE FOR PRESENTS       $: 100
EXCHANGE RATE ($ TO THE £)   : 2.05

POUNDS STERLING REQUIRED   £: 217.073171
*******************************************
```

Table 3.9   Output from 'Number of £s required' program

Problem 3 – Cost of stationery

Calculate the cost of stationery for a course that is being run, given the following information:

Number of delegates attending	58
Cost of folders	14p each
Cost of paper	26p per pad
Cost of pens	12p each

Allow two pens per delegate (there is a quantity discount of 8 % for orders over 100 pens). Write the program so that it may also be used on other occasions, when different numbers of delegates will be attending, and allow for changes in costs.

```
NO OF DELEGATES          : 58
COST OF FOLDERS          : 14 P EACH
COST OF PAPER            : 26 P PER PAD
COST OF PENS (LESS 8%)   : 12 P EACH

TOTAL COST OF STATIONERY = £ 36.0064
*******************************************
```

Table 3.10   Output from 'Cost of stationery' program

4 Program Development

4.1 The need for pre-planning

This chapter gives you guidance on developing a proposed program. If a program is written too hastily valuable time may be lost subsequently in implementing the necessary changes. Time spent pre-planning is seldom wasted. Commercial systems designers and programmers are expected to conform to a specific formal procedure. In developing your own programs, you need to exercise self-discipline.

4.2 Understanding the problem

The first step is to ensure that you understand what you intend or are required to do. Are the terms of reference clear? This might mean that you need to check the meaning of any terminology or jargon used. You may also need to ensure you understand the mathematical notation used to specify any relationships involved. Thus, initially, some research or background reading may be necessary. Research may also be necessary when you know what you want to do, but are not sure of the method to be used.

4.3 Designing output

The starting point of designing a program should be the output. You need to consider and make decisions on the following aspects.

The output from a program may be printed and/or written to a file. Is your output going to be solely printed, written to a file or a mixture of both? This leads on to deciding precisely what is to be printed and what is to be written to the file.

For example, your intention may be to write a program to read a stock data file and produce a list of items to re-order. Given, for the moment, that a program can be written to identify the items to be re-ordered, you need to consider: Should the output be solely a printed list or should a re-order file be produced that can be the input to a purchase order program? If you are going to have a printed list of items to be re-ordered, what should it contain? Should it list the complete stock record of each item or, the other extreme, should it just be a list of stock code numbers?

A program of this nature is developed in Chapter 11, in that case the re-order list consists of stock code and stock description. The whole record was not printed but only sufficient to fully identify each stock item.

Having decided what is to be output it is then necessary to consider the format and general layout. The considerations to be made are:

In which columns are the variables to be printed?

Should they be truncated or rounded?

Are column headings necessary?

Are main headings necessary?

What spacing is required between headings?

Should headings be underlined?

The output to a re-order list program might therefore start as shown in Table 4.1.

```
40 PRINT "RE-ORDER LIST"
45 PRINT "-------------"
50 PRINT
60 PRINT "CODE","DESCRIPTION"
65 PRINT "----","----------"
70 PRINT
```

Table 4.1   Headings for re-order program

4.4 Input requirements

Once the output details have been decided you can then identify the necessary input. If a large amount of data is to be processed it may be advisable to read it from a data file; this is dealt with further in Chapter 11. If the data is solely associated with the one program it can be incorporated in DATA statements, while data that varies from run to run is best entered via INPUT statements.

You may not be the only person using the program and this is a factor to be considered. Values should be entered in their most usual form, i.e. 12.5 not .125 for interest rates (see, for example, the mortgage problem in Chapter 12, p. 131). Ample print messages should be provided, giving guidance, if necessary, as to the input required.

A further aspect of the input design is the desirability of providing some form of control over the program during run time. For example, in the 'Heat of combustion' problem (Chapter 12, p. 117), the user is asked whether any more data is to be processed and replies Y or N, i.e.

100 PRINT "ANY MORE DATA (Y = YES, N = NO)";
110 INPUT Y$

4.5 Your BASIC system

Before considering the method of processing in detail, it is necessary to consider the BASIC statements you have available. This book presents the BASIC statements common to most systems. However, before you use any extensions available on your system you need to consider the likelihood of wishing to transfer your programs to another system.

4.6 Flowcharting

Once you have a broad idea of your requirements the logical sequence of the program statements needs to be developed.

Symbol	Use

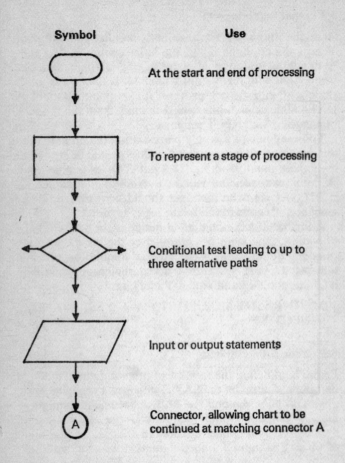

At the start and end of processing

To represent a stage of processing

Conditional test leading to up to three alternative paths

Input or output statements

Connector, allowing chart to be continued at matching connector A

Figure 4.1 Some flowchart symbols

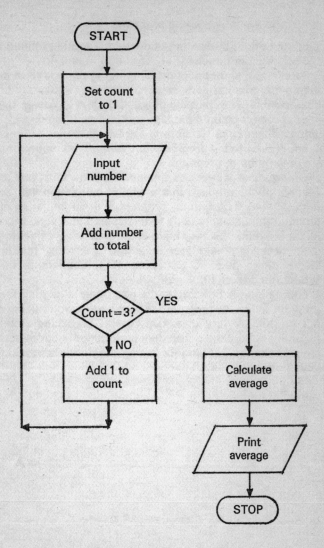

Figure 4.2 Flowchart for average of three numbers

This can be done by drawing a flowchart. The more common symbols used in flowcharts are shown in Figure 4.1.

An example of the use of the flowchart symbols is given in Figure 4.2, where it is required to calculate the average of three numbers. The purpose of a flowchart is to ensure the logic is correct before becoming involved with the detail of individual program statements. Further examples of flowcharts will be found elsewhere in this book accompanying the description of programs.

On occasions it becomes apparent from the flowchart or analysis of the problem that a similar calculation will be repeated several times in the program. When a similar set of program statements is likely to be required in several parts of the program, this may indicate the possibility of writing them once only as a *subroutine* and using this routine several times over. A discussion of subroutines is the subject of Chapter 10.

Having drawn flowcharts, the next stage is writing the program. When the program has been written, you still have not finished. A very important part of producing useful programs is to ensure that they perform as intended and the next chapter discusses the testing and documentation of your programs.

5 Program Testing

5.1 Purpose of program testing

As you have seen in Chapter 1, a computer only 'understands' programs written in its own machine code, which is made up of binary patterns. Therefore, your BASIC program has to be translated into the computer's binary code before the instructions contained within the program can be executed. This translation process is carried out by another machine code program called a BASIC compiler or interpreter. (See Chapter 1, p. 9.)

The BASIC system that you use will expect your programs to contain instructions which have been written according to a fixed set of rules. If you do not follow any of these rules, then the BASIC system will recognise this during the translation process and output a message indicating that a *syntax error* has occurred. Examples of syntax errors are given in section 5.2. All syntax errors must be corrected before you can proceed. When all the instructions are acceptable to the BASIC system, that is, no error messages are shown, the program may be run with data.

At this stage, only the correctness of the BASIC instructions has been achieved. The logic of the program may be in error and hence give wrong results or cause an *execution error* to occur. An execution error occurs when an instruction in the program asks the computer to perform an action which it cannot do. When this happens, the computer stops obeying any further instructions and outputs an error message giving an indication of why it had to stop executing the program. Examples of execution errors are given in section 5.3, and of logical errors in section 5.4.

The purpose of program testing is to achieve an error-free program which will produce correct results for all the data for which it has been designed.

So far the program instructions you have learnt are executed by the computer in the order in which you have written them. In Chapter 7, you will learn other BASIC instructions which will allow you to instruct the computer to execute different sets of instructions in your program, according to the results of certain tests. That is, you will be able to instruct the computer to 'jump' or branch to a different part of your program if, for example, the value of a variable is equal to, greater, or less than, some given value. This means the sequence of instructions obeyed using one set of data may be different from that using another set of data. You can only prove that your program is correct for all the data that may be used by designing your test data in such a way that *every* instruction path (a sequence of instructions) in your program can be obeyed. This is discussed further in section 5.4.

As the programs you write become more complex, it will become important for you to define the details of the problem, to analyse the structure of the program that is required, to show the logic in the form of a flowchart (as explained in Chapter 4, p. 31), to define the test data and the limits and format of the data that may be used with the program, and to describe the running of the program. At a later stage you may wish to change parts of the program and these amendments need to be recorded. All this information forms part of the program documentation which is discussed in section 5.6 below.

5.2   Syntax errors

The following sections give examples of typical syntax errors.

5.2.1 *Mistake in the spelling of a command*

This is most likely to occur when you input your program from the terminal and may be avoided, to some extent, by observing the display on the teletypewriter or visual display screen as you type the instructions. You then have an opportunity of correcting your mistakes before transmitting the instruction.

A typical example of this type of error is:

$$100 \text{ REED N}$$

where READ has been misspelt as REED.

This will cause an error message to be output either immediately under the instruction, or at the end of the program. (The methods of editing your BASIC program are discussed in Chapter 6.)

The error message that is output will vary according to the BASIC system used. For the example shown above the error message could be:

KEYWORD UNKNOWN

5.2.2 *Wrong instruction format*

Beginners sometimes make the following mistakes when writing an arithmetic statement for calculating, say, $\frac{118 \times 2.6}{5 \times 7.3}$ ($= 8.40548$) with the result assigned to C.

Wrong version

$$110 \text{ LET } 118 \times 2.6/5 \times 7.3 = \text{C}$$

Correct version

$$110 \text{ LET C} = (118*2.6)/(5*7.3)$$

That is, the corrections are:

Substitute * for × to indicate multiply.

Remember that the evaluation of the right-hand side of the equals sign is stored as the new value for variable C.

Use of brackets

Notice that brackets had to be inserted to cause the correct value to be assigned to C. Without brackets the instruction would be:

$$110 \text{ LET C} = 118*2.6/5*7.3$$

This is an acceptable BASIC instruction and no *syntax* error will be indicated. However, since the value assigned to C will be wrong ($\frac{118 \times 2.6}{5} \times 7.3 = 447.928$), this instruction will cause a *logical* error to occur.

5.2.3   *Wrong variable name*

As you learnt in Chapters 2 and 3, most BASIC systems only allow you to use the following variable names:

The single letters A–Z, and any of these single letters followed by any of the single numbers 0–9.

String variables consist of any of the single letters A–Z followed by a dollar sign (e.g. A$).

If you try to use a variable name which does not obey these rules (e.g. A10, AB or D1$), a syntax error will be indicated.

You may use a wrong variable name which will cause a *logical* error to occur but no *syntax* error. For example, the following LET statement is correct BASIC:

$$120 \text{ LET A} = B/D3$$

However, if D2 should have been used instead of D3, then the wrong value would have been assigned to A. If D3 had not been assigned a value before the above statement was executed, then most BASIC systems would assign zero to D3 and this would cause an *execution* error because dividing by zero gives infinity. Since it is impossible to store infinity in the computer, the above LET instruction could not then be executed.

5.3 Execution errors

There are several different types of execution error. Some typical examples are shown in the following sections.

5.3.1 *Calculated value not within range of computer*

A computer can only store numbers within a given range depending on the structure of its main store. Therefore, you will first need to find out what this range is for the computer you are using. You will then need to check that the BASIC instructions in your program do not cause values to be calculated which are outside this range (values which are either too small or too large) and hence give rise to arithmetic overflow. As you have seen in section 5.2, dividing by zero is an example which causes this type of execution error.

5.3.2 *Incorrect input data*

The data that you input must be suitable for assigning to the variables specified. For example, the following BASIC instruction is intended for reading a date in for later printing:

10 INPUT D

When the program is run interactively, a ? will be output to indicate that the required data (the date) should be typed in:

? "14/03/80" will cause an execution error.

The error message output could be:

BAD INPUT, RETYPE FROM ITEM 1

indicating that you should try to input the data again. However, the error is not in the data, but in statement 10 above. 27/03/80 may only be input into a string variable. If you amend statement 10 as follows:

10 INPUT D$

then the response "14/03/80" to ? is acceptable.

5.4 Logical errors

A logical error may either cause an execution error to occur, or will give wrong results during or at the end of the program execution.

In section 5.2.2 you saw that writing an arithmetic expression in correct BASIC will result in a logical error if the order of evaluation of the expression is not taken into account. Many logical errors are due to mistakes in arithmetic expressions, so these need to be checked carefully before the program is input into the computer. In addition, the results using test data must be checked against manual calculations to ensure that the program is working correctly. If the evaluation of a wrong arithmetic expression is a number outside the range of the computer, this will result in an execution error as stated in section 5.3.1.

Other logical errors will occur if the wrong instruction path is followed in the program, because the test selecting the path is wrong.

Figure 5.1 shows a flowchart for a program which has different instruction paths according to the results of tests in the program. The flowchart is logically correct for the problem stated below. In Chapter 7 you will learn how to write the BASIC program for it.

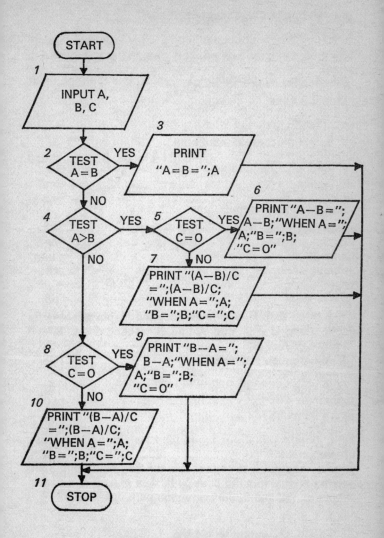

Figure 5.1 Flowchart for problem

5.4.1 *Problem*

Input three values and assign these to A, B and C. If A is greater than B, calculate $\dfrac{A - B}{C}$ unless C is zero, when you should output:

A — B = (the calculated value)
               WHEN A =   B =   C = 0

                    value input

If C is not zero output:

  (A — B)/C = (the calculated value)
               WHEN A =   B =   C =

                    value input

If A is less than B, calculate values and output as above for C = 0 and C ≠ 0, with A and B exchanged (i.e. B — A instead of A — B).
If A = B, then just output:

$$A = B = \text{(input value of A)}$$

5.4.2 *Effect of wrong tests*

If a mistake is made in any of the tests, this will result in a logical error.

For example, if the test at *2* in the flowchart (Figure 5.1) were wrongly specified as A > B, then if A, B and C were input as 5, 2 and 3, the instruction path would be:

1, 2, 3, 11.
That is, the output would be:
A = B = 5

Because B is not printed, it is not obvious that the output is logically incorrect. This is shown up if the input data is checked against the output, i.e. input data A = 5, B = 2, C = 3, output A = B = 5 !

If, in addition to specifying test *2* wrongly as A > B, the test at *4* were specified wrongly as A = B, using data A = 4, B = 4, C = 0 would result in the following output (instruction path is *1, 2, 3, 4, 5, 6, 11*):

$$A - B = 0 \quad \text{WHEN } A = 4 \quad B = 4 \quad C = 0$$

This appears logically correct, but it is not the required output as specified in the problem for the case when A = B.

If the tests at *2* and *4* were correctly specified but if the test at *5* and the print instruction at *6* were omitted, then using A = 8, B = 3 and C = 0 would cause the following instruction path to be followed:

$$1, 2, 4, 7, 11.$$

An attempt to obey the instruction at *7* would result in an execution error, because the evaluation of (A − B)/C would give infinity.

5.5 Preparing test data

As mentioned previously, the data you select for testing your program must test every instruction path. This will be illustrated using the problem given in section 5.4.1 and the flowchart in Figure 5.1.

There are five possible instruction paths in the problem as follows:

path 1: *1, 2, 3, 11*
path 2: *1, 2, 4, 5, 6, 11*
path 3: *1, 2, 4, 5, 7, 11*
path 4: *1, 2, 4, 8, 9, 11*
path 5: *1, 2, 4, 8, 10, 11*

Therefore five different sets of values for A, B and C are required to test the program fully. Table 5.1 shows the associated conditions for each path together with suitable test data and expected results.

Use simple numbers for the test data wherever possible to make the manual calculations used for checking easier. There is no point in using more test data than required; just use sufficient to test your program fully.

Path	Conditions	Data A B C	Expected results
1	$A=B$	4 4 0	$A=B=4$
2	$A>B, C=0$	8 3 0	$A-B=5$ WHEN $A=8$ $B=3$ $C=0$
3	$A>B, C\neq0$	5 2 3	$(A-B)/C=1$ WHEN $A=5$ $B=2$ $C=3$
4	$A<B, C=0$	6 10 0	$B-A=4$ WHEN $A=6$ $B=10$ $C=0$
5	$A<B, C\neq0$	3 7 2	$(B-A)/C=2$ WHEN $A=3$ $B=7$ $C=2$

Table 5.1   Test data for the program

5.6   Documentation

Whether you are developing a program for your own use or one that is to be used by other people, it is very important to write down details of the program and its use. The following notes indicate the type of information that you should include in your documentation. It is advisable to develop standards for your documentation so that the information is recorded in a similar way for each program; this will make it easier to follow and should ensure that all the essential factors are included.

Identification

The program or subroutine should be given a unique name, and this should be shown on the title page together with the programmer's name, location and the date of completion.

Contents page

All pages of the documentation need to be numbered. The name of each section should be shown on the contents page, with the appropriate page number, for easy reference to particular sections.

Summary

It is useful to have a short summary at the *beginning* of the documentation to show the function of the program and its limitations. The computer(s) on which the program was developed and run, and the programming language used can be included here or on the title page. In addition, the memory and peripherals (e.g. cassette recorder, card reader, printer) required for the program need to be specified. The summary should indicate concisely the usefulness of the program to the potential user.

Description of the problem

Details of the problem to be solved, but not the actual program, should be included in this section. Background information, such as mathematical formulae or tables, can be included here, or if extensive, reference can be made to appendices.

Specification of the program

The logic of the program may be described in words only if it is relatively simple. Usually, a flowchart is required, together with a written description. It is essential to ensure that the flowchart is up-to-date and matches the final program coding. The latter should be included as an appendix.

Input and output formats

Most programs process data which is input at run time. The data that the program can process will be of a certain format. For example, numeric data needs to be specified as a range of numbers comprising a certain number of integral and decimal places. The size of strings and the characters that may be included within the strings must be given. The program may have been written to reject data outside these limits, or an execution error may occur if data of the wrong format is input.

The output from the program will usually be in the form of a report. This may be just a single line of results, a table, a graph, or several lines (or pages) of information. In each case, the output needs to be specified in detail giving the possible types of character (numeric, alphabetic, special) that may be displayed or printed in certain positions on the screen or printer stationery.

There may be several different types of output from one program, and each needs to be identified and specified. Examples of each type of output should be shown in appendices and referenced in this section; these examples could be the results of your final test runs.

For programs using files of records, the different record and file formats should be specified in separate sub-sections.

Use of program

The details of how the program may be used should include the preparation of input data prior to running the program, the method of loading the program, run and any other commands required to operate the program on a particular computer.

If the input data is to be entered at run time from the keyboard, users should be encouraged to write these down in the required format to avoid wrong entries being made.

The test data that was used for the program should be given in an appendix in the form required for input; this enables the user to carry out a trial run to obtain the sample outputs given in the appendices.

Interpretation of outputs

The interpretation of the outputs with reference to the test data will help the user to understand the function of the program fully and to determine whether modifications are required.

Modifications

Many programs require modification after they have been in use for some time, in the light of the experience gained and because new circumstances have arisen. It is essential to include these modifications in the documentation when they have been carried out. This means showing modifications to the flowchart, logic description and program coding, and revised test data.

Appendices

As indicated earlier, appendices are used for detailed information that is referenced in the main part of the documentation, such as background details, program listings, output examples and test data. In addition, a list of operating instructions, and a list of error messages and their meaning should be included.

6 System Commands

6.1 Introduction

Some typical commands used in the development and running of BASIC programs are explained in the following sections. However, as these commands vary considerably from system to system you will also need to refer to the manuals for your particular system.

The logging in procedure described below is relevant to those using terminals linked to an interactive computer. If you are using a microcomputer you must first find out how to prepare the computer to accept BASIC programs.

The last section of this chapter specifies the types of modification required to run a BASIC program using batch processing.

6.2 Logging in

As soon as your terminal is connected to a computer, a response, such as the name of the computer service and date, may be printed at your terminal. Alternatively, this response might have to be initiated by yourself by typing in a specified character, e.g. a question mark (?).

After the computer has identified itself, it is usual for it to request your usercode (for charging purposes), and your password as shown below:

```
?
THE XYZ COMPUTER CO
ACCOUNT NO ——— 123,45
PASSWORD
```

The printing of your password is usually inhibited by the operating system , by pressing a control key on the terminal or a mask is printed to make the password unreadable. Both your code and your password must be accepted by the computer system before you can continue. If these are not accepted, then a message will be sent from the computer to the terminal stating this and you may be allowed a few more attempts before being disconnected.

When the usercode and password have been accepted, there is a further response from the computer to establish the language to be used. A typical query and response might be:

SYSTEM – BASIC

to which the computer responds,

READY

From this point on you are able to use the computer for developing, saving and running BASIC programs using commands of the type discussed in the following sections.

At the end of the computer session you disconnect from the computer by entering BYE (alternatives may be LOGOUT, OFF).

6.3 Creating and running a program

To clear the main memory ready for a program the command NEW is usually used. In some systems this can be followed by a program name, i.e.

NEW PROGA

where PROGA is the name of the program.

After a suitable response from the computer – e.g. READY – the BASIC program is then entered at the terminal. When the program has been entered, the command RUN will begin execution of the program at its first instruction.

If you wish to stop the program during execution you press the appropriate STOP or BREAK key. A command such as CONT (continue) can be entered to allow the run to continue.

6.4   File handling

A program entered via the terminal is in the main memory and will be lost when you disconnect unless you save it on the secondary store (disc or tape, depending on the system).

The command SAVE (or SAVE PROGA) will cause a copy of the current program to be recorded on a file under the name specified (PROGA). On some systems whenever a program name is specified, it may need to be enclosed within, say, quotation marks.

On a later occasion, when you have logged in, the command OLD PROGA will cause the file named PROGA to be copied into the main memory. An alternative command might be LOAD PROGA.

If your system allows you to erase files by system commands then the command is usually either UNSAVE PROGA or SCRATCH PROGA. Systems having these features might also allow you to replace an existing version of the program (or file) by an amended one that is currently in the main memory by the command REPLACE PROGA. Alternatively, if you initially copied PROGA into main memory from a file by means of OLD PROGA and you have now altered it and wish to save the *revised version* under a different *name* the command RENAME PROGB can be used. This will cause only the program in the main memory to be renamed, it can then be SAVED. You will then have two filed versions of the program, PROGA and PROGB.

6.5 Program development and editing

When a program has been entered into the main memory it is useful to be able to inspect all or part of it. This is done by the LIST command.

LIST by itself will cause the whole program to be listed at the terminal. Specified lines can be listed, i.e. LIST 120 will cause line number 120 to be printed. A block of lines can be listed, e.g. LIST 120–150 will cause lines 120–150 to be printed. LIST –150 would be interpreted as list from the beginning up to line 150 while LIST 150– would list from line 150 to the end.

Using the above command any part of a BASIC program can be inspected. To change a line, the line is simply re-entered, the revised line automatically overwriting the previous version in the main memory.

Similarly, to add a line it is entered via the keyboard. (It must have a unique number otherwise it will overwrite an existing line.)

To delete lines, only the line number need be entered (i.e. you are overwriting an existing line with an empty line). Alternatively, and especially when a block of lines is involved, the command DELETE might be available (e.g. DELETE 120–150).

After modifying programs in this way, your line numbers may be very erratic and, furthermore, you may wish to insert a line between say, lines 173 and 174. Some systems have a command that will renumber all the lines either starting at 100 in steps of 10 or in a manner you specify. This command is typically RENUMBER, or RE-SEQUENCE.

The more elaborate systems might allow you to combine two existing files into one in the main memory by the command MERGE. This command requires the files involved to be specified and will usually combine them end on in the sequence specified, i.e.

MERGE PROGA, PROGB

A RENUMBER is therefore often appropriate after a MERGE.

6.6 Batch processing

Control instructions are usually required when submitting a BASIC program for batch processing. For example, *B preceding the first instruction could indicate to the computer system that the program is in BASIC. Other system commands may also be necessary to determine the identification of the user and the nature of the run. A terminator (e.g. *) may be required after the last BASIC instruction, which is usually an END statement.

Data associated with INPUT statements has to be available for reading on the appropriate peripheral device when the program is executed.

7 Conditional and Unconditional Branching

7.1 Controlling the order in which instructions are obeyed

For most problems the computer needs to be programmed to *repeat* a set of instructions and to execute different sets of instructions in the program according to the requirements for that particular run. This is done by means of *branch* (jump instructions).

The GOTO instruction causes control to pass to the line number in the statement. That is, the computer will execute next the statement it has branched to and continue to execute the instructions following in sequence until it encounters another branch instruction. For example:

$$50 \text{ LET I} = 1$$
$$60 \text{ PRINT I}$$
$$70 \text{ LET I} = \text{I} + 2$$
$$80 \text{ GOTO } 60$$

will cause the odd numbers 1, 3, 5 etc. to be printed. When the computer executes the instruction at line 80, it will always branch to line 60 and obey that instruction followed by line 70. Therefore, the GOTO statement is an unconditional branch instruction, since it is always executed independently of any condition that exists.

However, you will notice that in the above section of a program, there is no instruction which stops the program being executed; it will go on for ever!

To stop the computer executing this set of instructions, you will need to insert a conditional branch instruction. This will perform a test to see if a condition exists and pass control to a different part of the program according to the result of the test.

A conditional branch instruction that you may use in BASIC is the IF . . . THEN statement. For example, to stop the program which prints odd numbers, you could insert the following instructions:

$$65 \text{ IF } I = 21 \text{ THEN } 90$$
$$90 \text{ END}$$

Try running the program and see if it stops after 21 has been printed. If you replace 21 by an even number, say, 20 or 22, the program will not stop since I never has this value.

7.2 Loops and their control

The small program that you have just tested has a set of instructions, lines 60–80, which are performed repeatedly, thus forming a loop. The flowchart for this program shows the loop and the branch out of the loop more clearly (see Figure 7.1). Notice the GOTO 60 instruction is represented by an arrow from box 70 to box 60.

There are several alternative ways of exiting from a loop and for branching to different parts of a program. The format of the IF . . . THEN statement is:

line number IF *relational expression* THEN *different line number*

Notice that the line number following the THEN *must* be different from the line number preceding the IF, otherwise the IF statement itself will cause continuous looping.

The relational expression is the test that is to be performed. If this test is true (that is, the condition exists), then control passes to the line number following the THEN. If the test is false, then control passes to the line number following the IF statement, that is, the instructions will

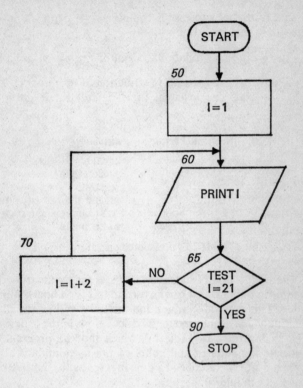

Figure 7.1 Flowchart to illustrate loop control

continue to be obeyed in sequence until another branch
instruction is met.

The relational expression compares two expressions, so
that its format is:

expression relational operator *expression*

You have already used one relational operator in the
previous example = (equal to). The full list is given in
Table 7.1.

relational operator	meaning
=	equal to
>	greater than
<	less than
>= or =>	greater than or equal to
<= or =<	less than or equal to
<> > or ><	not equal to

Table 7.1 Relational operators

The IF . . . THEN statement is useful for terminating the
reading in of data, as it can be used to test for a final dummy
value. This is a value which indicates the end of the data
list, but which is not used in the calculations in the program.
This is illustrated in Table 7.2, which shows a program to
calculate the squares and cubes of positive numbers. The
numbers are entered one at a time in response to the INPUT
statement in line 30.

The program in Table 7.2 will stop when either a zero or
a negative value is read into X. The IF . . . THEN statement
must appear before the calculations involving X, so that the
dummy value is not used in the calculations.

Another way to stop repetition of a set of instructions is to
specify the number of times the loop has to be carried out.
For example, the program in Table 7.3, will read and output
N numbers, where the first number to be read is N.

```
10 PRINT "SQUARES AND CUBES OF POSITIVE NUMBERS"
11 PRINT
20 PRINT " X "," S"," C"
30 INPUT X
40 IF X < = O THEN 90
50 LET S = X*X
60 LET C = S*X
70 PRINT X,S,C
80 GOTO 30
90 END
```

Table 7.2 Terminating with a dummy value

If line 30 in Table 7.3 read:

$$30 \text{ LET I} = 1$$

then line 70 would need to be:

$$70 \text{ IF I} < = \text{N THEN } 40$$

This is because the value of I, after line 60 has been obeyed, is one greater than the number of numbers when the loop has been executed N times, if I is set to 1 to start with. This means the loop is terminated when $I = N + 1$.

```
10 INPUT N
20 PRINT "READ";N;"NUMBERS"
25 PRINT
30 LET I = 0
40 INPUT X
50 PRINT X
60 LET I = I + 1
70 IF I < N THEN 40
80 END
```

Table 7.3 Program to read and output N numbers

7.3 A program using conditional statements

You can now practise using IF . . . THEN statements, and the testing of a program with a number of different branches, by coding the problem given in Chapter 5, section 5.4.1. You should have the flowchart in front of you when you code the BASIC program. Test the program with the data given in Table 5.1, p. 44 *before* you enter it in the computer (this is known as *dry-running* a program). This will enable you to spot logical errors in your coding, and you are also likely to find a few mistakes in your BASIC statements which would lead to syntax errors. This method of working usually results in a correct program being obtained sooner. Use all five sets of test data in one run of the program by inserting another loop which terminates when the input data for A, B and C are all zeros. The calculations may form part of the PRINT statement as indicated in the flowchart. For example, the result of A — B does not need to be stored but can be calculated and printed in the same statement as follows:

$$110 \text{ PRINT ``A} - \text{B} =\text{''};\text{A} - \text{B}$$

The program is listed in Table A4, p. 138.

7.4　Comparing character strings

The IF . . . THEN statement may also be used to compare character strings, since each character is represented by a unique combination of binary digits when stored in the computer. For example, if P$ contains the character H, then:

$$25 \text{ IF P\$} = \text{``H''} \text{ THEN } 30$$

will be true and a branch will be made to line 30.

This facility is particularly useful for comparing names, addresses and similar information for business applications. You will need to refer to a list of codes used to represent characters in your computer's memory to find out which characters have a lower or higher value for greater than or less than tests. The ASCII 64 character set is given in Appendix C.

7.5 The FOR ... NEXT statements

In section 7.2, the number of times a loop was executed was
programmed by setting an initial value for the loop counter,
testing for a final value, and incrementing the current value
of the loop counter if the final value had not been reached.
The FOR ... NEXT statements have been designed to
program these three operations in an easier way.

In the example to read and output N numbers, on p. 56,
the variable I (used as the loop counter) was set to an initial
value 0. 1 was added to I after the number had been read
and output, and finally a test was carried out $(I < N)$ to
determine whether the program should loop back or stop.
FOR ... NEXT statements will be used in an alternative
version of the program. The FOR ... NEXT statements
consist of two lines of code. At the beginning of the loop
the FOR statement is used to set up the initial conditions,
the increment or STEP to be made at the end of the loop
and the final value as follows:

line number FOR *variable = expression 1* TO *expression 2*
STEP *expression 3*

where expression 1 sets the initial value of the loop counter
(also known as the index), expression 2 sets the final value of
the loop counter, and expression 3 gives the increment to be
added to the variable at the end of each pass through the set
of instructions in the loop. If the STEP is equal to 1, both
the word STEP and expression 3 may be omitted.

The final instruction in the loop has the format:

line number NEXT *variable*

where the variable has the same name as that given in the
associated FOR statement.

The program in Table 7.3 can be amended as shown in
Table 7.4. A number will be read into X and output N times
as controlled by the FOR ... NEXT statements. I is set to 1

initially in line 30, then in line 60 I is incremented by 1 and if it is greater than N the program will go to line 80 and stop, otherwise it goes back to line 40.

```
10  INPUT N
20  PRINT "READ";N;"NUMBERS"
25  PRINT
30  FOR I = 1 TO N
40  INPUT X
50  PRINT X
60  NEXT I
80  END
```

Table 7.4 Alternative program to read and output N
numbers

Insert the instruction:

70 PRINT I

so that you can see the value of I after the loop has been executed for the required number of times.

You may use I within the loop, but you should avoid changing I (that is assigning a new value to I) within the loop as this changes the conditions set up by the FOR ... NEXT statements. The problem flowcharted in Figure 7.1 may be coded as follows:

```
50 FOR I = 1 TO 21 STEP 2
60 PRINT I
70 NEXT I
80 END
```

The value of the increment given in the expression following STEP may be negative (so that the loop counter is decremented) or fractional. There are a number of rules governing the use of FOR... NEXT statements. The program in Table 7.5 includes various outcomes as shown in Table 7.6, which you should test on your computer.

Notes on Tables 7.5 and 7.6

1   Changing initial, final and step values has no effect on the number of loops executed (lines 200–250). However, changing the index within the loop causes the conditions used to control the FOR loop to be changed as seen in lines 270–300. The loop is performed four times instead of sixteen times.

2   At line 350 when I reaches 6, the expression $A*I = B$ is true, and a branch is made to outside the loop (i.e. to line 380).

3   If the final value is not hit, then it will be exceeded as in lines 400–420. X has values 5, 15, 25, 35; the final value given in line 400; i.e. 30 stored in B, is not reached after three passes through the loop and is exceeded on the fourth pass.

7.6   The ON ... GOTO statement

The IF ... THEN statement is available with all standard BASIC interpreters and compilers. However, extended BASIC statements have been implemented in many cases to give you additional facilities. One such statement is the ON ... GOTO statement.

The format of the ON ... GOTO statement is

line number ON *expression* GOTO *two or more line numbers separated by commas*

The integral part of the evaluated expression must be a positive number not greater than the *number* of line numbers after the GOTO part of the statement.

Control will pass to the first, second, third, etc. line number after the GOTO if the integral part of the expression is equal to 1, 2, 3, etc.

For example, different calculations may need to be carried out according to a code, as in the following problem. A

```
10  PRINT "STEP NEGATIVE TO DECREMENT"
20  FOR I = 5 TO 1 STEP −1
30  PRINT I
40  NEXT I
45  PRINT
50  PRINT "STEP FRACTIONAL"
60  FOR A = .75 TO 2.25 STEP .5
70  PRINT A
80  NEXT A
82  PRINT
85  PRINT "SAME INITIAL VALUE AND STEP"
90  READ J,K,L
100  DATA 10,40,5
110  FOR I = J TO K STEP J
120  PRINT I
130  NEXT I
135  PRINT
140  PRINT "MORE COMPLICATED EXPRESSIONS"
150  FOR I = J + K TO J∗K + J + K STEP J↑2
160  PRINT I
170  NEXT I
175  PRINT
```

Table 7.5 (1)   Program to illustrate rules for FOR ... NEXT
statements

STEP NEGATIVE TO DECREMENT
 5
 4
 3
 2
 1

STEP FRACTIONAL
 .75
 1.25
 1.75
 2.25

SAME INITIAL VALUE AND STEP
 10
 20
 30
 40

MORE COMPLICATED EXPRESSIONS
 50
 150
 250
 350
 450

Table 7.6 (1)   Output from program given in Table 7.5 (1)

```
180 PRINT "CHANGE INITIAL,FINAL AND STEP"
190 PRINT "VALUES WITHIN LOOP"
200 FOR I = J TO K STEP L
210 PRINT J,K,L
220 LET J = J + 1
230 LET K = K - 10
240 LET L = L/2
250 NEXT I
255 PRINT
260 PRINT "CHANGE INDEX VALUE IN LOOP"
270 FOR I = 1 TO 16
280 LET I = I + 3
290 PRINT I
300 NEXT I
305 PRINT
310 PRINT "BRANCH OUT OF LOOP"
320 READ A,B
330 DATA 5,30
340 FOR I = 1 TO 10
350 IF A*I = B THEN 380
360 PRINT I
370 NEXT I
380 PRINT A,B,I
385 PRINT
390 PRINT "FINAL VALUE NOT HIT"
400 FOR X = A TO B STEP 10
410 PRINT X
420 NEXT X
430 END
```

Table 7.5 (2)   Program to illustrate rules for FOR . . .
NEXT statements

```
CHANGE INITIAL,FINAL AND STEP
VALUES WITHIN LOOP
 10               40              5
 11               30              2.5
 12               20              1.25
 13               10              .625
 14                0              .3125
 15              -10              .15625
 16              -20              7.8125E-2

CHANGE INDEX VALUE IN LOOP
  4
  8
 12
 16

BRANCH OUT OF LOOP
  1
  2
  3
  4
  5
  5               30              6

FINAL VALUE NOT HIT
  5
 15
 25
```

Table 7.6 (2) Output from program given in Table 7.5 (2)

number of sets of data are to be input. Each set consists of a code (1, 2, 3, 4 or 5) and values of X and Y. Calculations are to be performed on each set of data according to the rules shown in Table 7.7.

Code	Calculation
1	R = X + Y
2	R = X — Y
3	R = X*Y
4	R = X/Y
5	R = X↑Y

Table 7.7 Calculations for different codes

You can now write a program to tabulate the code, the X and Y values, and the results of the calculations.

Use the ON ... GOTO statement to control which calculation is to be carried out according to its associated code. Draw a flowchart for the program, prepare test data, code and run your BASIC program. Remember the test data must test every branch in your program. You may input the codes and data in any order, that is the first set of data may have a code of, say, 3, the next a code of 1, etc. Compare your program with the one listed in Table A5. Suitable test data and calculated values are given in Appendix B.

7.7 Further use of the TAB function and FOR loops

The TAB function may be used with a variable or expression in the brackets following TAB, e.g. TAB(I), TAB(P — 1). The program given in Table 7.8 outputs a rectangle of variable dimensions, consisting of L1 dashes for the two lines across the L2 ↑s for the two vertical lines.

Notes on Table 7.8

1 Lines 20 and 40 output a message to the user asking for data to be entered. This is useful when the program is being run interactively, but should be omitted for batch running unless you are testing for subsequent interactive working.

```
20 PRINT "ENTER START COLUMN POSITION";
30 INPUT P
40 PRINT "ENTER LENGTH ACROSS AND DOWN";
50 INPUT L1,L2
55 PRINT
60 LET K = 1
70 PRINT TAB(P − 1);
80 REM FOR LOOP TO OUTPUT DASHES ACROSS
90 FOR I = 1 TO I1
100 PRINT "−";
110 NEXT I
120 PRINT
130 IF K = 2 THEN 240
140 REM NESTED FOR LOOPS TO OUTPUT "↑"S DOWN
150 FOR I = 1 TO L2−2
160 PRINT TAB (P − 1);"↑";
170 FOR J = 1 TO L1−2
180 PRINT " ";
190 NEXT J
200 PRINT "↑"
210 NEXT I
220 LET K = K + 1
230 GOTO 70
240 END
```

Table 7.8 Program to output a rectangle

2 The PRINT statement in line 70 is terminated by a semi-colon (;); this will cause the *next* PRINT statement that is obeyed to output on to the *same* line.

3 Line 120 is necessary to cause the complete line of L1 dashes to be output. After passing through line 220, which sets K to 2, lines 90–120 are repeated to complete the rectangle and execution of the program is then terminated.

4 Lines 150–210 comprise a FOR loop which has another FOR loop (lines 170–190) wholly within it. The FOR loops are said to be *nested* and this will be discussed further in Chapter 9. For each pass through the outer FOR loop, the inner loop is executed L1–2 times, so that a ↑ is output followed by some spaces and then another ↑. When line 190 is reached another pass through the outer loop is executed until L2–2 lines, consisting of ↑ spaces ↑, have been output.

In this case, the use of nested FOR loops could be avoided by replacing lines 160–200 by the following statement:

160 PRINT TAB(P − 1); "↑"; TAB(L1− 1 + P); "↑"

Figure 7.2 shows a rectangle output by the program when the following data was used:

$$7$$
$$24, 10$$

i.e. twenty-four dashes were output for the two lines across and eight ↑s for the two vertical lines.

You should enter the program given in Table 7.8 into your computer and run it with different input data.

7.8 PAGE and clear screen

Execution of the first PRINT instruction in a program usually causes the output to appear on the screen or printer below the end of the program listing.

For some purposes, the output needs to be displayed starting at the top of the screen, so that, for example, a table or a graph of results can be seen clearly. Other applications require a skip to be made to a new page of printed stationery at different stages during the execution of the program. For example, in problem 2, section 7.9, letter headings need to be printed at the top of each page, and similarly for the label print-outs.

The BASIC instructions for clearing the screen or skipping to the top of a new page are not standard, so you will need

Figure 7.2 Rectangle output from program

to find out the instructions that are available on your system. For problem 2, section 7.9, the instruction PAGE is shown in the listing (Table A6) whenever a skip to the top of the next page is required.

7.9 Problems

The following problems all refer to the name and address program given in Table 2.1, p. 17.

Problem 1 – Print options

Amend the program in Table 2.1 to allow selection of any combination of the three print options:

code	option
H	Letter heading
N	Notebook label
L	Envelope label
F	Stop execution of program

The amendments are given in Table A6.

Problem 2 – Letter headings

Amend the program in Table 2.1 to enable the letter heading print position and the number of headed sheets required to be entered at run time. The amendments are given in Table A7.

Problem 3 – Notebook labels

Amend the program in Table 2.1 so that the name in N$ is output centrally in a complete border of asterisks. Allow for the number of labels required, the length of the name, and the number of labels to be output per page to be entered at run time. The amendments are given in Table A8.

Problem 4 – Envelope labels

Amend the program in Table 2.1 to enable the total number of labels required and the number of labels per page to be entered at run time. The amendments are given in Table A9.

Note: Loops will need to be inserted into the program for problems 2, 3 and 4 to cause the required number of letter headings, notebook and envelope labels to be printed.

8 Functions

8.1 Library functions

Commonly used routines, such as those required for obtaining the integral part of a number (INT), the logarithm and antilogarithm of a number (LOG and EXP), and trigonometric functions (e.g. SIN) are available in BASIC. The functions contained in the built-in library vary according to the implementation of a particular BASIC system. Some systems include formatting functions, such as TAB, and also string functions. Examples of a variety of these functions will be given in the following sections. You will need to check their availability on your computer.

Further background on mathematical functions and problems involving these are given in *The Pocket Calculator* L. R. Carter and E. Huzan, Teach Yourself Books, 1979.

8.2 Arguments

Each function name is followed by an expression (the argument) in brackets. The function operates on the argument, that is, the value of the expression is used in the standard routine represented by the function name. For example:

$$100 \text{ LET } S = SQR(B*B - 4*A*C)$$

will evaluate the square root of the expression in brackets, i.e. $B^2 - 4AC$, and put the result in cell S.

There may be restrictions regarding the values of the argument associated with a function. For example, it is not possible to take the square root of a negative number, there-for the argument used with SQR must not have a negative value. The TAB function followed by a semicolon causes characters to be output in the column following the argument value; therefore, this value must correspond to a possible column position. A comma in place of the semicolon will have a different effect.

8.3 Using library functions

Library functions are used in LET or PRINT statements on their own or in expressions of any complexity. These expressions may contain further library functions. The evaluation is, as usual, working from the innermost brackets outwards.

8.4 Truncation

You have already used the library function INT to obtain the integral part of a number which has decimal places. The INT function gives the largest integer which is not greater than the argument. Therefore, if the argument is a *positive* number, the decimal places are dropped and the number is said to be truncated after INT has been used. For example:

$$110 \text{ LET } B = \text{INT}(A)$$

puts 15 into B if A is 15.36. Remember A will remain unchanged after the LET statement has been obeyed, so it will still contain 15.36.

However, if A contains −15.36 then the integer placed into B is *not* −15 (since this is larger than −15.36) *but* −16; in this case, B does not contain the truncated value of A.

To obtain the truncated value of a *negative* number, the sign must be removed from the number before the INT function is applied, using the function ABS which takes the absolute value of its argument (i.e. the sign is ignored), and the function SGN used. SGN gives the value of 1 if its argument has a positive value, -1 if its argument has a negative value, and zero if the value of its argument is zero. For example:

$$120 \text{ LET } B = SGN(A)*INT(ABS(A))$$

multiplies the integral part of the absolute value of A by its sign, so that B will contain the truncated value of A when A is positive or negative. Assuming A contains -15.36, as in the previous example, then ABS(A) gives 15.36, INT(ABS(A)) gives 15, and SGN(A)*INT(ABS(A)) multiplies 15 by -1 giving -15.

8.5 Rounding

Numbers often need to be rounded to a nearest number of decimal places or to a nearest value in general. Adding 0.5 to a number before truncating it will cause the number to be rounded to the nearest integer (whole number). For example:

$$130 \text{ LET } B = INT(A + 0.5)$$

puts 24 in B if A contains, say 24.3, and 25 in B if A contains, say 24.5 or 24.6. The program shown in Table 8.1 illustrates this method of rounding; angles input in decimals of a

```
20  PRINT "    ANGLE    DEGS    MINS"
30  PRINT
40  INPUT A
50  IF A = 0 THEN 110
60  LET D = INT(A)
70  REM ROUND TO NEAREST MINUTE
80  LET M = INT((A − D)*60 + 0.5)
90  PRINT TAB(3) ;A;TAB(12) ;D ;TAB(19) ;M
100 GOTO 40
110 END
```

Table 8.1 Rounding to nearest minute

degree are output in degrees and minutes, rounded to the nearest minute.

To round a number to a certain number of decimal places, you need to divide the number by a scaling factor before adding 0.5, truncating, and finally multiplying by the scaling factor. For example, to round to three decimal places the scaling factor is 0.001:

140 LET P2 = INT(P1/0.001 + 0.5)*0.001

puts 3.142 into P2 when P1 contains 3.14159.

In general, if the scaling factor is contained in F then an expression may be rounded by using:

$$INT((\text{expression})/F + 0.5)*F$$

This will work also if, for example, you wish to round a number to the nearest 10; in this case, F = 10.

8.6 Square roots

The library function for obtaining a square root is SQR. Remember the argument must not have a negative value. You can use SGN to test the sign, as shown in Table 8.2.

The program given in Table 8.3 calculates and outputs the diameter in metres (rounded to two decimal places) of

```
70  INPUT N
80  FOR I = 1 TO N
90  INPUT A,B,C
100 LET R = B*B − 4*A*C
110 IF SGN(R) = −1 THEN 150
120 LET R = SQR(R)
130 PRINT "SQUARE ROOT =";R; "FOR ";A;B;C
140 GOTO 160
150 PRINT "RESULT NEGATIVE FOR ";A;B;C
160 NEXT I
170 END
```

Table 8.2 Use of SGN and SQR

cylindrical tanks, given the volume V (in litres of water) and three standard heights in metres. The formula for the volume of a cylinder of height h, and radius r is:

$$V = \pi r^2 h$$

Therefore, the diameter d is given by:

$$d = 2r = 2\sqrt{\frac{V}{\pi h}}$$

```
20 PRINT "     VOLUME   HEIGHT    DIAMETER"
30 PRINT "     LTRS.     M.        M."
40 PRINT " - - - - -   - - - - -   - - - - - - - -
50 DATA 1,1.25,1.75
60 INPUT V
80 IF V = 0 THEN 160
85 PRINT
90 FOR I = 1 TO 3
100 READ H
110 LET D = INT(SQR(V/(1000*3·142*H))*200 + 0.5)/100
120 PRINT TAB(4);V;TAB(14);H;TAB(24);D
130 NEXT I
140 RESTORE
150 GOTO 60
160 END
```

Table 8.3 Calculation of diameter of cylindrical tanks

In the problem, the three standard heights are given in a DATA statement. For each volume V the diameter D is calculated and output using each of the three standard heights in turn. Every time the READ H statement (line 100) is obeyed, the next value in the DATA statement is taken. That is, the first time through the FOR loop H is taken to be 1, the second time 1.25, and the third time 1.75. The DATA pointer then needs to be reset to the beginning of the DATA values ready for a further three passes through the FOR loop with the next value of V. This is achieved by the RESTORE statement in line 140. Use the program to find the diameter of tanks which have volumes of 500 and 1000 litres (1000 litres = 1 m³). The answers are shown in Table 8.4.

VOLUME LTRS.	HEIGHT M.	DIAMETER M.
500	1	.8
500	1.25	.71
500	1.75	.6
1000	1	1.13
1000	1.25	1.01
1000	1.75	.85

Table 8.4   Output from program given in Table 8.3

8.7 Trigonometric functions

The sine, cosine and tangent of angles are obtained by using the function names SIN, COS and TAN respectively, followed by the angle in brackets (expressed in radians). For example:

$$100 \text{ LET } X = COS(B)$$

will put the cosine of B (radians) in cell X.

Only the inverse tangent (arctangent) is usually available as the function ATN. This has as the argument the tangent of the required angle. The angle obtained will be in radians $-\pi/2$ to $\pi/2$.

For angle x, $\tan x = \dfrac{\sin x}{\cos x}$ and $\sin^2 x + \cos^2 x = 1$.

Therefore, the inverse sine and inverse cosine of x may be expressed as follows:

$$\sin^{-1}x = \tan^{-1}\left[\frac{\sin x}{\sqrt{(1 - \sin^2 x)}}\right] \qquad \ldots (8.1)$$

$$\cos^{-1}x = -\tan^{-1}\left[\frac{\cos x}{\sqrt{(1 - \cos^2 x)}}\right] \qquad \ldots (8.2)$$

When $0 < x < \pi/2$ cosines are positive $= \cos x$
When $\pi/2 < x < \pi$ cosines are negative $= -\cos(\pi - x)$

Equation (8.2) is true for both cases. When $\cos x > 0$, the expression in brackets ($= \cos x$) is positive and equation (8.2) gives the required angle as x. When $\cos x < 0$, the expression in brackets is negative and equation (8.2) gives the required angle as $\pi - x$.

The following BASIC statements may be used to find angle A in radians given that the sine of the angle is S or the cosine of the angle is C:

    110 LET A = ATN(S/SQR(1 − S∗S))
    120 LET A = − ATN(C/SQR(1 − C∗C)) + 1.5708

where $\pi/2 \simeq 1.5708$
Note: You must avoid using the above formulae when $S = 1$ (required angle is $\pi/2$) or $C = 1$ (required angle is 0).

π may be available as a library function with some systems. If π is not available, its numeric value may be used as a constant. Alternatively, ATN(1)∗4 will calculate π, since the tan of $\pi/4$ radians is 1.

8.8   Logarithms and antilogarithms

The logarithms and antilogarithms of expressions are given by the functions LOG and EXP, respectively. For example, the xth root of a number may be found by dividing the log of the number (y) by x and taking the antilog; this may be expressed as shown in the following BASIC statement:

$$100 \text{ LET R} = \text{EXP(LOG(Y)/X)}$$

After this statement has been obeyed, R will contain the required root.

The function LOG gives the logarithm of its argument to

base e; these are known as Naperian (or natural) logarithms. Since,

$$\log_{10} y = \frac{\log_e y}{\log_e 10}$$

the following BASIC statement finds the log of a number (Y) to base 10:

110 LET T = LOG(Y)/LOG(10)

Similarly, the antilog is found by multiplying the log to base 10 by $\log_e 10$ and taking the antilog of the result as follows:

120 LET A = EXP(T*LOG(10))

e has the value 2.7182818 to 8 significant figures. The function EXP raises e to the Xth power, where X is its argument. That is, $EXP(X) = e^x$; the use of EXP is illustrated further in the next section.

8.9   Hyperbolic functions

Hyperbolic functions may be expressed in terms of e^x. For example:

$$\sinh x = \frac{1}{2}(e^x - e^{-x})$$

$$\cosh h = \frac{1}{2}(e^x + e^{-x})$$

$$\tanh x = \frac{\sinh x}{\cosh x} = \frac{e^x - e^{-x}}{e^x + e^{-x}}$$

The sinh of the number held in cell X will be placed into cell Y by the following LET statement:

110 LET Y = (EXP(X) − EXP(−X))/2

8.10 TAB function

The TAB function has already been used in several examples. The definition of TAB is summarised below. The TAB function may only be used in PRINT statements to give the next output column position.

If TAB(P) is followed by a semicolon, then the variable or expression following the semicolon will be output starting at column INT(P+1) for most systems. P may be any expression, but TAB(P) has no meaning if it tries to position the output to a column beyond the available output positions or to a column before the current position in the line.

For example, if P has the value 200, and only 80 output positions are available, then TAB(P) will either have no effect or produce an error. Similarly, if in the current PRINT statement TAB(20);A; has been used where A occupies 3 columns, then a subsequent TAB(22) in the same PRINT statement has no meaning because the output is already past column 22.

8.11 String functions

These functions return the length of a string (LEN), substrings of a specified length and position from a named string (LEFT$, RIGHT$, and MID$). Other functions may be used to convert from one representation to another, for example, ASC returns a numeric code which is the equivalent of a specified character (the reverse function, numeric code to character is given by the function CHR$).

These functions are particularly useful when dealing with files and are described more fully in Chapter 11.

8.12 Random numbers

Pseudo random numbers may be obtained by the use of the function RND. This function chooses a number at random between 0 and 1. This facility can be used in programs to form the basis of chance outcome in games, and to simulate randomness in scientific and business applications.

The numbers generated are not truly random (they are pseudo random), each successive number being arithmetically related to the previous one. This usually means that if a program is rerun the same sequence of 'random' numbers will be generated. In some systems the function is RND(X), where X is a dummy number having any value. The value of X may determine the starting point of the string of numbers generated, that is, RND(7) will generate a difference sequence from RND(3). However, because RND(7), for example, is fixed within a program the same sequence will be generated each time the program is run. To overcome this, some systems allow an initialising instruction of RANDOMIZE to be used. Each computer run will then start from a different initial 'seed' number.

The random numbers generated will usually need to be manipulated. For example, to represent the throw of a die integer values between 1 and 6 need to be randomly generated. This may be done with the following instruction:

$$100 \text{ LET } T = \text{INT}(6*\text{RND} + 1)$$

The $+1$ is required as otherwise the truncated integer would lie between 0 and 5.

When it is required to generate numbers to represent a sample from a uniform distribution a single statement similar to the above will be sufficient. In more advanced cases of simulation, it is often required to sample from a given frequency distribution. A subroutine suitable for these circumstances is described in Chapter 10.

8.13 User defined functions

You may define your own functions by using a DEF FNx statement, which has the following format:

line number DEF FN*x*(*variable*) = *expression*

Each user-defined function must have a unique name within the program as given by FNx, where x is any alphabetic letter A–Z.

Each function has a dummy argument given by the variable in brackets above. The actual argument used when the function is subsequently referenced in the program will be different from the dummy argument in the function definition. For example, the previous expression used to round a number can now be defined as a function as follows:

$$50 \text{ DEF FNR(A)} = \text{INT(A/F} + 0.5)*\text{F}$$

This can be used subsequently in the same program to round a number to, say, the nearest 100 and to one decimal place as shown in Table 8.5.

```
50  DEF FNR(A) = INT(A/F + 0.5)*F
60  READ B,C
70  DATA 650,32.55,649,32.54,651,32.56,0,0
80  IF B = 0 THEN 190
100 REM ROUND B TO NEAREST 100
110 LET F = 100
120 LET B1 = FNR(B)
130 REM ROUND C TO 1 DECIMAL PLACE
140 LET F = 0.1
150 LET C1 = FNR(C)
160 PRINT "B =";B;"B1 =";B1,"C =";C;"C1 =";C1
170 PRINT
180 GOTO 60
190 END
```

Table 8.5 Program to round numbers

A user-defined function may contain another user-defined function in its definition. For example, the program given in Table 8.6 tabulates the sines of a number of angles (given) and the corresponding angles expressed in degrees to two decimal places.

```
20 PRINT "   SINE    DEGREES"
30 PRINT "   - - - -   - - - - - - -"
40 PRINT
50 DEF FNR(A) = INT(A/.01 + 0.5)*.01
60 DEF FND(U) = 180/(ATN(1)*4)
70 DEF FNA(S) = (ATN(S/SQR(1 — S*S)))*FND(U)
80 INPUT X
90 IF X = 0 THEN 160
100 IF X <> 1 THEN 130
110 LET D = 90
120 GOTO 140
130 LET D = FNR(FNA(X))
140 PRINT TAB(5) ;X ;TAB(15) ;D
150 GOTO 80
160 END
```

Table 8.6 Sines and angles (in degrees)

8.14 Problems

Problem 1 – Radius of circumcircle

Write a program to find the radius of a circular track passing through points which form a triangle. The radius (r) of the circumcircle of a triangle is given by:

$$r = \frac{a}{2\sin A} = \frac{b}{2\sin B} = \frac{c}{2\sin C}$$

where a, b, c and A, B, C are the sides and angles of the triangle.

The program is listed in Table A10, and the answer for $a = 452$ metres, $b = 386$ metres and $c = 739$ metres is given in Appendix B. (*Note:* $\cos B = (a^2 + c^2 - b^2)/2ac$.)

Problem 2 – Areas of triangles

The area of a triangle, with sides a, b and c and angles A, B and C, may be calculated if the three sides *or* two sides and the included angle are given, by using one of the following formulae:

$$\text{area of triangle} = \sqrt{(s(s-a)(s-b)(s-c))}$$
$$\text{where } 2s = a + b + c$$

or   area = ½absin C or ½bcsin A or ½acsin B

Write a program to tabulate the areas of the triangles given in Table 8.7, using suitable headings. Note *unknown* values have been set to zero. Output all areas in square cm to one decimal place. The program is listed in Table A11, and the answers are given in Appendix B.

| | Sides of triangle (cm) | | Included angle |
	a	b	c	(degrees)
	17.2	9.8	14.1	0
	0	74	98	125.4
	292	0	405	30.5
	10.3	15.6	0	69
dummy values—1	0	0	0

Table 8.7   Data used to calculate areas of triangles

Problem 3 – Volumes of solids

The volume of a solid of uniform cross-sectional area (A) and height (H) is given by:

$$V = A \times H$$

The uniform cross-sectional areas of some common solids are given in Table 8.8 together with their codes.

Write a program to calculate the volumes of the solids given in Table 8.8. All dimensions are in cm. The name of the solid is to be held in a DATA statement. Output the name of the solid and its volume. Code 0 can be used to terminate execution of the program. Suitable test data is given in Table 8.9, but include some extra data of your own.

Code	Solid	Cross-sectional area
1	cuboid	$L \times W$
2	cylinder	$\pi \times R^2$
3	hexagonal bar	$\frac{1}{2}\sqrt{27} \times D^2$

L = length   W = width   R = radius   D = length of side

Table 8.8   Some solids with uniform cross-sectional areas

Code	1st dimension (L or R or D)	2nd dimension (W or zero)	Height (H)	Required no. of decimal places
2	4.5	0	1.75	2
3	12.6	0	250	0
1	5.3	7.0	4.2	1

Table 8.9   Data for 'Volumes of solids' problem

The program is listed in Table A12, and the answers are given in Appendix B. The program presented in Table A12 allows the user to round the answer using a scaling factor (F) to give the required number of decimal places (see section 8.5).

9 Arrays

9.1 Lists and tables

So far single memory cells have been referenced by single variable names. This allowed a total of 286 names to be used for storing numbers and twenty-six names for storing character strings.

Many problems involve processing a number of variables in exactly the same way. In these programs, it is much more convenient to use the same name to reference a number of memory cells whose contents are processed by the same set of instructions in the program; a subscript is used in association with the variable name to identify uniquely each particular memory cell. For example, the program given in Table 9.1 inputs a list of N numbers and outputs a list of numbers that are greater than 10, and a list of numbers that are negative, using two passes through the stored data.

If N is equal to 9, then the list of 9 numbers is input into memory cells A(1), A(2), ..., A(9), since in the FOR loop (lines 20–40) I takes the values 1–9. I is the subscript and A is the name of an array of nine elements. Each element of the array may be referenced by the array name and the subscript referring to its position in the array. That is, A(4) refers to the fourth number input into the array A, which is the memory cell between those occupied by A(3) and A(5).

Most BASIC systems start numbering the elements of an array at 0, that is, the first element of the array is referenced by A(0). The program given in Table 9.1 may be amended so that it can be used to input and process nine numbers starting at A(0) by changing the initial value of I to 0 in each FOR statement, lines 20, 70 and 140. N would need to be input as 8 instead of 9 in this case.

```
10 INPUT N
20 FOR I = 1 TO N
30 INPUT A(I)
40 NEXT I
50 PRINT "NUMBERS GREATER THAN 10"
60 PRINT
70 FOR I = 1 TO N
80 IF A(I) < = 10 THEN 100
90 PRINT A(I)
100 NEXT I
110 PRINT
120 PRINT
130 PRINT "NEGATIVE NUMBERS"
140 FOR I = 1 TO N
150 IF A(I) > = 0 THEN 170
160 PRINT A(I)
170 NEXT I
180 PRINT
190 END
```

Table 9.1   Program to output numbers >10 and negative numbers

Try running the program given in Table 9.1 with the following nine numbers:

$$6, 12, -30, 10, -4, 47, 9, 0, 58$$

The output for this data is shown in Table 9.2.

Array A, in the previous example, is called a one-dimensional array because it has one subscript. Many BASIC systems allow up to three subscripts, that is one-, two- or three-dimensional arrays. A one-dimensional array is a list, and a two-dimensional array is a table. A three-dimensional array is more difficult to visualise; an example would be to have the page number of a book as the third dimension (subscript), and the lines and columns on a page forming a table referenced by the other two subscripts. The subscripts are separated by commas within the brackets following the name of the array, so that T$(3,2,8) could refer to the third line and second column on the eighth page of a book.

NUMBERS GREATER THAN 10

```
12
47
58
```

NEGATIVE NUMBERS
```
—30
—4
```

Table 9.2 Output from program given in Table 9.1

9.2 Naming arrays

Arrays used for holding numbers must be called by a single letter of the alphabet, A–Z, followed by the subscripts in brackets. There are, therefore, twenty-six possible array names that may be used for storing numbers. Similarly, character strings may be stored in arrays, and these must be called by a single alphabetic letter, A–Z, followed by a $ sign and the subscripts in brackets.

Array names which are identical to single variable names may be used in the same program. That is, the BASIC system will distinguish between A used as a single variable and A (subscript(s)) used as an array element for storing numbers, and A$ used as a single string variable and A$ (subscript(s)) used for storing character strings.

9.3 Subscripts

The one, two or three subscripts that may be used with array names may consist of any expression. However, since the subscripts refer to unique positions in the array which is stored in memory cells in the computer, the individual subscripts must have positive values which the system will truncate to integer values. Zero is a possible value for a subscript in some BASIC systems as explained previously.

The integer values of the subscripts must lie within the bounds of the array. For example, in the program given in Table 9.1 the BASIC system automatically allocates eleven memory cells (subscripts 0–10) in the absence of a DIM statement, which will be explained in the next section. If N were input as, say, 20 then elements referenced in the FOR statement beyond the A(10) element would be outside the defined storage of the array (i.e. outside the bounds of the array); in this case an execution error would occur.

9.4 The DIM statement

The DIM statement is used to define storage for arrays which have subscripts whose values are greater than ten. Although the DIM statements can appear anywhere in the program (before the array is accessed) it is better to place it at the beginning of the program so that it is separate from the main logic.

The format of the DIM statement is:

line number DIM *list of array variables separated by commas*

The array variables in the list may be ordinary or string variables; each variable name is followed by up to three subscripts, separated by commas, in brackets.

For example, array X is to be used to store a list of up to fifty numbers, and array T$ is to be used to hold a table comprising a maximum of 5 rows and 7 columns.

The DIM statement to define storage for these two arrays is:

$$30 \text{ DIM } X(50), T\$(5,7)$$

X will have fifty-one memory cells of storage reserved referenced by X(0), X(1), X(2), ..., X(50). T$ will have a total of forty-eight cells reserved, the first cell being referenced by T$(0,0) and the last cell by T$(5,7).

Notice that storage is reserved for the *maximum* array size in each case. A particular run of your program may require less storage than the maximum; this is acceptable or alternatively you can input values for the variable subscripts in the DIM statement before it is used (this is known as dynamic dimensioning). Dynamic dimensioning is not available on every BASIC system; note that the dimensioning may only be done *once* during the program run. For example, the DIM statement below requires K, L and M to be input at run time.

40 DIM X(K),T$(L,M)

More than one DIM statement may be used in a program, but the *same* array name may *not* appear in more than one DIM statement in a program. For example:

50 DIM B$(30,8),A$(60),A(20,20)⎫
60 DIM D(100),C$(5,7,6)　　　　 ⎬correct

is correct.

70 DIM B$(30,8),A$(60),A(20,20) ⎫
80 DIM D(100),A(20,20),C$(5,7,6)⎬incorrect

will produce an error because A(20,20) appears in the DIM statements in line 70 *and* in line 80.

It is important to note that the DIM statement may be used to override the automatic storage allocation for small arrays. For example, if array A is to contain a maximum of six cells and array B a maximum of four cells, then DIM A(5),B(3) will cause the *exact* storage required to be allocated, thus *saving* storage compared with the automatic allocation of eleven cells for each array.

9.5   Nested FOR loops

A FOR loop may lie wholly within another FOR loop, as was shown in Table 7.6, Chapter 7. This facility is particularly useful for manipulating arrays. For example, the data given in Table 9.3 is to be input into a two-dimensional array called A and output in the form shown in Table 9.4. The program given in Table 9.5 uses nested FOR loops to achieve this; try running this program.

1	2	3	4
5	6	7	8
9	10	11	12

Table 9.3   Input data for 'Nested FOR loops' program

1	5	9
2	6	10
3	7	11
4	8	12

Table 9.4   Table to be output

```
10  DIM A(3,4)
20  DATA 1,2,3,4,5,6,7,8,9,10,11,12
30  FOR I = 1 TO 3
40  FOR J = 1 TO 4
50  READ A(I,J)
60  NEXT J
70  NEXT I
80  FOR I = 1 TO 4
90  FOR J = 1 TO 3
100  PRINT A(J,I) ;
110  NEXT J
120  PRINT
130  NEXT I
140  END
```

Table 9.5   Program using nested FOR loops

9.6 Problems

Write programs for the following problems.

Problem 1 – Copying an array

Copy an array A comprising N elements into an array B, of the same size as A, in reverse order. For example, if N is 20, A(20) will go into B(1), A(19) into B(2), etc. Assume N is always a multiple of 5, and output array B in rows of 5 columns (positions 7, 13, 19, 25 and 31).

The program is listed in Table A13.

Problem 2 – Sum of elements

Sum the elements on the diagonals of an M × M array. Allow for M to be odd (as well as even) when the central element must be added in only *once*. Test your program in one run with an odd *and* an even value for M. Output the array and the sum of the elements on the diagnoals in each case.

The program is listed in Table A14.

Problem 3 – Sorting a list of numbers

Sort a list of N numbers, held in array A, into ascending numerical order. Use only *one* array which is *just* large enough to hold the maximum number of numbers that may be input. The logic of the method is shown in Figure 9.1. This involves pushing the highest number to the end of the list by exchanging the higher number of each pair working through the list. That is, if element A(1) is greater than element A(2) then their contents are exchanged so that the higher value is in A(2); then the value in A(2) is compared with that in A(3) and exchanged if necessary. The second pass through the list is shorter since at the end of the first

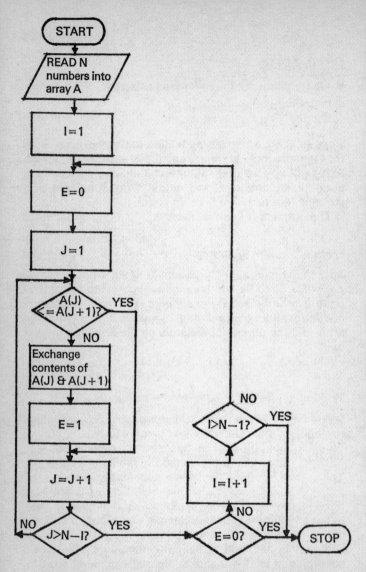

Figure 9.1 Sorting a list of numbers into ascending order

pass A(N) contained the highest value in the list and does not need to be compared again. If no exchanges take place during a pass (i.e. E = 0) then the list is in the required sorted order and no further passes are necessary.

Output the list of numbers in its original order and after each pass of the sort so that you can see how this sorting method works. Use the following data, and create your own data, to provide a variety of different lists to be sorted.

Data:

15, 12, 3, 20, 22, 22, 9, 4, 23, 2, 0, −25, 17, 18

The program is listed in Table A15. The output from the program for the above data is shown in Table 9.6.

15	12	3	20	22	22	9	4	23	2	0	−25	17	18
12	3	15	20	22	9	4	22	2	0	−25	17	18	23
3	12	15	20	9	4	22	2	0	−25	17	18	22	23
3	12	15	9	4	20	2	0	−25	17	18	22	22	23
3	12	9	4	15	2	0	−25	17	18	20	22	22	23
3	9	4	12	2	0	−25	15	17	18	20	22	22	23
3	4	9	2	0	−25	12	15	17	18	20	22	22	23
3	4	2	0	−25	9	12	15	17	18	20	22	22	23
3	2	0	−25	4	9	12	15	17	18	20	22	22	23
2	0	−25	3	4	9	12	15	17	18	20	22	22	23
0	−25	2	3	4	9	12	15	17	18	20	22	22	23
−25	0	2	3	4	9	12	15	17	18	20	22	22	23

Table 9.6 Sorting a list of numbers

10 Subroutines

10.1 Purpose of subroutines

A subroutine is a sequence of instructions designed to perform one or more specific tasks. The routine may be required more than once in different places in the program. When a routine is written as a subroutine it is incorporated in the main program once. During execution the statement, GOSUB *linenumber*, causes control to pass to the line number specified. Execution continues until a RETURN statement is encountered. Control then passes back to the statement *following* the originating GOSUB statement.

A subroutine can be entered as many times as required and therefore can save the writing of similar instructions in several parts of the program. Apart from the extra program writing, the program usually becomes longer if subroutines are not used. A longer program requires more computer storage, and takes longer to translate into machine code; using subroutines wherever possible generally makes a program more efficient.

Once a subroutine has been developed and tested it may be used in quite different programs, either as it stands or with modifications. If possible, subroutines should be designed to allow them to be used in many different ways without modification. This may be done by building in flexibility.

10.2 Independent development

Another advantage of using subroutines is that they may be developed and tested independently from the program(s) in which they are to be used.

By testing subroutines independently a complex program may be built up more quickly using *proved* subroutines. In addition, if a subroutine has been developed for one program, then it can be tested with suitable test data for use in a different program *before* it is incorporated. However, the final program will need to be tested as a *whole* to ensure that the linkages, i.e. statements between the subroutines (as well as the subroutines), give correct results for every branch of the program. The test data must be comprehensive enough to test *every* instruction in the program, as discussed in Chapter 5.

10.3 Graphs and histograms

If you use a computer to analyse data it is almost certain that at some time you will want to plot the data, or maybe group it into a frequency table. The following sections describe a series of subroutines that allow you to do this.

To allow the subroutines to be compatible we need to standardise some of the variable names. The routines have been written to allow up to 100 data values to be processed. These values will be held in the array V. There is therefore the need for a DIM V(100) in the main program. If the data is to be grouped into a frequency table before, say, printing out a histogram, the variable will be stored in array X and the frequency in array F. A frequency table having a maximum of fifteen class intervals should be adequate for most purposes. Therefore the main program will need a DIM statement containing X(15), F(15).

10.4 Serial plotting routine

A routine to plot a series of values sequentially is useful for time series based data. The examination of the graph might confirm that it is not worthwhile using more elaborate analyses to seek non-existent trends, or seasonal patterns.

A plotting routine is given in Table 10.1. The largest value to be plotted (M) is found (lines 1110–1150) and from this the scaling factor is calculated. Line 1160 has been written to fit the maximum value within thirty print positions. This could be altered depending on the available

```
1010  PRINT
1020  PRINT "NO OF DATA POINTS =";N
1030  PRINT
1040  PRINT "ENTER NO OF POINTS TO PLOT";
1050  INPUT Q
1060  IF Q > N THEN 1010
1070  LET B = 1
1080  IF Q = N THEN 1110
1085  PRINT
1090  PRINT "START PLOT AT DATA POINT NO";
1100  INPUT B
1105  LET Q = Q + B −1
1110  LET M = 0
1120  FOR I = B TO Q
1130  IF V(I) < M THEN 1150
1140  LET M = V(I)
1150  NEXT I
1160  LET S = 1 + INT(M/30)
1170  PRINT
1180  PRINT "ONE PLOT POSITION =";S;"UNITS"
1190  PRINT
1200  PRINT " N DATA";
1210  PRINT TAB(9) ;"0";TAB(17) ;10*S;TAB(27) ;20*S
1220  PRINT TAB(9) ;"I....:....I....:....I....:...."
1230  FOR I = B TO Q
1240  LET K = INT(V(I)/S + .5)
1250  IF K > 0 THEN 1280
1260  PRINT I;TAB(5) ;V(I) ;TAB(9) ;"*"
1270  GOTO 1290
1280  PRINT I;TAB(5) ;V(I) ;TAB(9) ;"I";TAB(K + 9) ;"*"
1290  NEXT I
1300  PRINT TAB(9) ;"I....:....I....:....I....:...."
1310  PRINT
1320  RETURN
```

Table 10.1 Serial plotting routine

characters per line. The first ten print positions are taken up by the data point number (N) and the actual value V(I).

Problem 1 – Plot of percentage pastureland

Write a program using the above routine to plot the reducing percentage pastureland, as given in Table 10.2. The program is given in Table A16, and the output in Table 10.3.

Year	% Pastureland
1	82
2	72
3	63
4	60
5	57
6	54
7	50
8	45
9	38
10	35

Table 10.2 Pastureland in a parish

10.5 Frequency grouping subroutines

Before producing a histogram, or carrying out other forms of analysis, it is often required to group individual data points into class intervals and note the total number of values falling into each interval (i.e. the frequency).

A subroutine to do this is given in Table 10.4. The frequency table so constructed is composed of fifteen class intervals. Any data not included as a result of this constraint is printed out by line 2100. A new run can then be undertaken with the class interval parameters respecified accordingly.

ENTER NO OF YEARS ? 10

% PASTURELAND, YR 1 ? 82
% PASTURELAND, YR 2 ? 72
% PASTURELAND, YR 3 ? 63
% PASTURELAND, YR 4 ? 60
% PASTURELAND, YR 5 ? 57
% PASTURELAND, YR 6 ? 54
% PASTURELAND, YR 7 ? 50
% PASTURELAND, YR 8 ? 45
% PASTURELAND, YR 9 ? 38
% PASTURELAND, YR 10 ? 35

ENTER NO OF POINTS TO PLOT ? 10

ONE PLOT POSITION = 3 UNITS

```
 N    DATA  0         30        60
             I....:....I....:....I....:....
 1     82   I                              *
 2     72   I                          *
 3     63   I                      *
 4     60   I                     *
 5     57   I                    *
 6     54   I                   *
 7     50   I                 *
 8     45   I              *
 9     38   I           *
10     35   I          *
             I....:....I....:....I....:....
```

BREAK IN 120

Table 10.3 Percentage pastureland output

```
2000  PRINT "ENTER SIZE OF CLASS INTERVAL";
2010  INPUT C
2015  PRINT
2020  PRINT "ENTER LOWER BOUND OF 1ST. INTERVAL";
2030  INPUT L
2040  FOR I = 1 TO N
2050  FOR J = 1 TO 15
2060  IF V(I) > = (L + (C*J)) THEN 2090
2070  LET F(J) = F(J) + 1
2080  GOTO 2110
2090  NEXT J
2100  PRINT V(I) ;"NOT COUNTED"
2110  NEXT I
2120  FOR J = 1 TO 15
2130  LET X(J) = L + ((J − .5)*C)
2140  NEXT J
2150  RETURN
```

Table 10.4 Frequency grouping routine

The reason for designing the program in this manner is that a completely automatic parameter setting routine may disguise the presence of a 'rogue' value which, once pointed out, you are happy to ignore.

A subroutine to print out a frequency table is given in Table 10.5. As this subroutine is intended to be independent

```
3000  PRINT
3010  LET C = X(2) − X(1)
3020  LET L = X(1) − (.5*C)
3030  PRINT"- - - - - - - - - - - - - - - - - - -"
3040  PRINT TAB(4) ;"X";TAB(14) ;"F"
3050  PRINT "- - - - - - - - - - - - - - - - - - -"
3060  FOR I = 1 TO 15
3070  LET B = L + C*(I −1)
3080  PRINT B ;TAB(4) ;"−";TAB(14) ;F(I)
3090  NEXT I
3100  PRINT "- - - - - - - - - - - - - - - - - - -"
3110  RETURN
```

Table 10.5 Frequency table routine

of the grouping subroutine, the class interval and lower
bounds are calculated from the array values of X.

The third subroutine in this set outputs the frequency
table in histogram form. The program is given in Table 10.6.
As with the plotting routine it has been written to use thirty
print positions for the histogram. To change the number of
print positions from thirty, lines 4250, 4260, 4300, 4350 and
4475 need to be changed accordingly.

```
4000 LET M = F(1)
4010 PRINT
4020 PRINT
4210 FOR I = 2 TO N
4220 IF F(I) < M THEN 4240
4230 LET M = F(I)
4240 NEXT I
4250 IF M > 30 THEN 4300
4260 LET U = INT(30/M)
4265 LET S = 1/U
4285 PRINT U;" STARS = 1 UNIT"
4290 GOTO 4330
4300 LET S = INT(M/30)
4302 IF S > 0 THEN 4310
4304 LET S = 1
4320 PRINT "ONE STAR = ";S;" UNITS"
4330 PRINT
4350 PRINT"CLASS";TAB(7);"I....:....I....:....I....:....I"
4400 FOR I = 1 TO N
4410 LET K = INT((F(I)/S) + .5)
4412 IF K > 0 THEN 4420
4414 PRINT I;TAB(7);"*"
4416 GOTO 4470
4420 PRINT I;TAB(7);"I";
4430 FOR J = 1 TO K
4440 PRINT "*";
4450 NEXT J
4460 PRINT
4470 NEXT I
4475 PRINT TAB(7);"I....:....I....:....I....:....I"
4480 PRINT
4490 RETURN
```

Table 10.6   Histogram routine

Problem 2 – Pastureland histogram

Write a program incorporating these subroutines to process the data shown in Table 10.7. The output required is a frequency table and histogram of the percentage pastureland.

Parish	% amount of pastureland
1	46
2	47
3	63
4	74
5	76
6	26
7	37
8	39
9	35
10	43
11	52
12	59

Table 10.7   Parish data

The program, which gives the output shown in Tables 10.8 and 10.9, is listed in Table A17.

10.6   Sampling from a frequency distribution

A subroutine is described below that allows a value to be sampled from a frequency distribution. The frequency distribution is contained in the two-dimensional array X. The first dimension contains the variable value, the second dimension contains the cumulative percentage frequency.

To allow the subroutine to be used generally in a variety of programs some standardisation of the array containing the frequency distribution is necessary. The number of class intervals has been set at 10 resulting in the dimensions for the array X being (10,2). Note that, for convenience, the existence of 0 subscripts have been ignored. If a required

```
.................
    X         F
.................
   20 –       1
   30 –       3
   40 –       3
   50 –       2
   60 –       1
   70 –       2
   80 –       0
   90 –       0
  100 –       0
  110 –       0
  120 –       0
  130 –       0
  140 –       0
  150 –       0
  160 –       0
.................
```

Table 10.8   Frequency table for Problem 2

```
 10   STARS = 1 UNIT
CLASS  I....:....I....:....I....:....I
  1    |*********
  2    |*************************************
  3    |*************************************
  4    |******************
  5    |*********
  6    |******************
  7    *
  8    *
  9    *
 10    *
 11    *
 12    *
       I....:....I....:....I....:....I
```

Table 10.9   Histogram for Problem 2

distribution contains less than ten rows (i.e. class intervals), the final entries in the array will be identical. For example, the data to be sampled, shown in Table 10.10, would be contained in the array X(R,I) as shown in Table 10.11.

Variable	Cumulative % frequency
5	10
10	27
15	42
20	65
25	80
30	100

Table 10.10   Data to be sampled

		Column subscript, I	
		(,1)	(,2)
	(1,)	5	10
	(2,)	10	27
	(3,)	15	42
	(4,)	20	65
	(5,)	25	80
Row subscript, R	(6,)	30	100
	(7,)	30	100
	(8,)	30	100
	(9,)	30	100
	(10,)	30	100

Table 10.11   Contents of X(R,I)

Any distributions to be used from a main program are established in a similar (10,2) format and array X can be equated to them before entering the subroutine.

10.7   Description of subroutine

A flowchart for the subroutine is shown in Figure 10.1 and
the listing is given in Table 10.12.

```
900  REM SAMPLING SUB
910  LET Z = 100*RND(3)
920  FOR R = 1 TO 10
930  LET V = X(R,1)
940  IF Z <= X(R,2) THEN 980
950  NEXT R
960  PRINT"ERROR : RN NOT PROPERLY ALLOCATED"
970  STOP
980  RETURN
```

Table 10.12   Sampling routine

The random number generated is scaled to lie between 0
and 100 (line 910). Within the FOR loop the array X is
inspected row by row. The value of the current row variable
is assigned to V (line 930) and the value of the scaled random
number Z is compared with the current cumulative frequency
(line 940). If Z is greater than the frequency the process is
repeated for the next row (line 950). When, eventually, the
random value Z falls within the current class interval the
subroutine is left, carrying back the current value of the
variable V. If, due to errors in setting up the distribution,
the random value Z cannot be associated with any particular
row then lines 960 and 970 are encountered, giving rise to
the error message.

A simulation program using this subroutine is given in
Chapter 12, section 12.5.

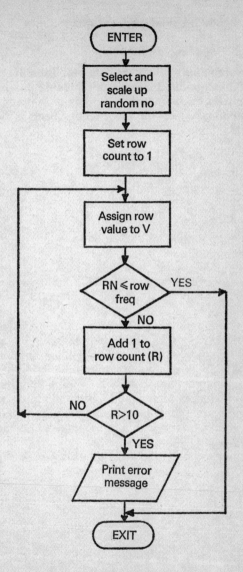

Figure 10.1 Sampling flowchart

Problem 3 – Input subroutine

Write a subroutine to allow the details of Table 10.10 to be entered into a two-dimensional array D. Make provision for up to ten rows to be entered.

A subroutine to meet the above requirements is shown in Table A18.

11 Using Data Files

11.1 Data files

When a large amount of common data is required by a program it is inconvenient to enter this data each time via the keyboard. A preferable method is to store the data in DATA statements within the program, as described in Chapter 3. However, this is still restrictive as these DATA statements are not readily available to other programs. The most flexible approach is to store your data in separate files from your programs so that the data files may be used by more than one program. You can then also prepare standard programs to analyse and process different data set up in data files.

A data files is created by a BASIC program so that the contents and format are under your control. In practice this means you are likely to write several programs, e.g. one to create the data file, one to update the data file, and some to process the data. This chapter shows how such data files may be created and read.

There are two ways of processing files: sequentially and randomly. Random access of files can only be carried out from discs, whereas sequential access can be carried out from disc or magnetic tape. This book deals only with sequential file systems.

11.2 File records

The contents of a data file may be regarded as the equivalent of a series of DATA statements within a program. Although the data consists of one long 'column' of values, it is useful for you to think and design the logic of your program round the concept of records. For example, a stock record might consist of a stock number, item description, stock level, unit cost and re-order level as shown in Table 11.1.

Stock No	Description	Stock	Unit Cost	Re-order level
1234	Pens	15	45	20
2340	Pencils	50	12	40
2679	Erasers	8	5	10
3456	Rulers	20	26	30
4567	Writing pads	40	35	50
4568	Note books	60	40	30
6770	Labels	70	15	25
6775	Pins	40	15	20
6979	Envelopes	40	20	60
7050	Cash books	30	22	40

Table 11.1 Stock Records

The data contained in Table 11.1, recorded sequentially record by record, would give rise to a 'column' of values as shown below:

> 1234
> PENS
> 15
> 45
> 20
> 2340
> PENCILS
> 50
> etc.

In transferring this data to and from memory it is more convenient to assign separate variable names to each part of a record and move one record at a time. This keeps the program logic simpler, although within a particular program a variable (unit cost, say) may not be manipulated or used.

As the program examples in this chapter use the data shown in Table 11.1, this is a convenient place to define the variable names to be used:

$$K = \text{stock number}$$
$$D\$ = \text{description}$$
$$S = \text{stock}$$
$$C = \text{unit cost}$$
$$R = \text{re-order level}$$

11.3 File declaration statements

This is one of the least standardised areas of BASIC and you need to check for the equivalent statements on your system.

Usually any files to be used by your program need to be declared before use. This declaration statement results in a file being assigned a number and subsequent file statements refer to the file by this number. Two common declaration statements are FILES and OPEN.

The FILES statement takes the form:

line number FILES *filename, filename, filename etc.* i.e.
10 FILES STOCK, TRANS

In the remainder of the program the file STOCK is file number 1 and TRANS file number 2 etc.

Alternatively, your system may require OPEN statements. These are of the general form:

line number OPEN *x, y, z, "filename"*

where *x, y, z* are file parameters as follows:

$x =$ the file number, as chosen by the user for this particular program
$y =$ the number of the device containing the file
$z =$ an indicator stipulating whether the file is to be opened to be read, or to be written to

E.g.   10 OPEN 2,1,1,"STOCK"

indicates that a file named "STOCK" will be referred to subsequently as file 2 and is located on device number 1. Where $z = 1$, this might indicate the file is to be written to.

The default option, OPEN x, usually means that the next file encountered will be opened to read only and will be assigned the number x.

A separate OPEN statement is required for each file being used. Each file that is opened also needs to be closed after final processing of the file by a CLOSE statement, e.g.

$$90 \text{ CLOSE } 1$$

11.4   File input–output statements

The statements used to read from or write to a file vary among the systems, although in all cases the file number forms part of the statement. The three most common alternatives are given below:

 WRITEFILE *filenumber, variable list*
 WRITE # *filenumber, variable list*
 PRINT # *filenumber, variable list*
e.g. PRINT # 1,K,D\$,S,C,R

The format in which the variable list is transferred to the file varies among systems. For example, the comma as a delimiter might be suppressed so that in the above example K,D\$,S,C,R, might be written as one string. If your system does this, then a way to preserve the variables separately is to use separate PRINT statements, i.e.

$$\begin{array}{l} \text{PRINT \# 1,K} \\ \text{PRINT \# 1,D\$} \\ \text{PRINT \# 1,S} \\ \text{PRINT \# 1,C} \\ \text{PRINT \# 1,R} \end{array}$$

or it might be possible to retain the commas by enclosing them in quotes, i.e.

PRINT # 1,K;",";D$;",";S;",";C;",";R

The corresponding read statements are:

READFILE, *filenumber, variable list*
READ # 1, *filenumber, variable list*
INPUT # 1, *filenumber, variable list*

Thus a corresponding read statement might be:

INPUT # 1,K,D$,S,C,R

11.5 End of file records

It is convenient if you have within your program your own means of detecting the end of your data. This can easily be done by terminating your data files with a dummy record. The contents of this dummy record is chosen to make it unique. For example, in the stock record file previously discussed the dummy stock number could be made larger than any likely to be encountered, i.e. 9999 if four-digit codes are used.

Since a complete record is transferred as a whole, the remaining fields of the dummy record need to be provided with values as shown below:

9999,X,0,0,0

The general flow of processing when a dummy record is used is shown in Figure 11.1.

Problem 1 – Stock data file

Write a program to create a stock data file incorporating a dummy end record for the data in Table 11.1.

A suitable program is listed in Table A19.

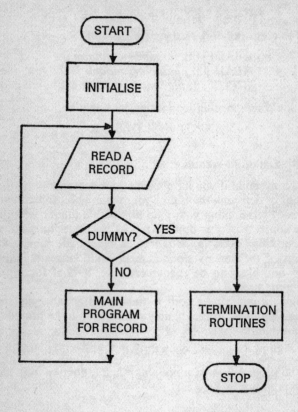

Figure 11.1 General flow with dummy record

Problem 2 – Re-order list

Write a program to read the data file produced in problem 1 and output a list of items to be re-ordered. A sample output is shown in Table 11.2.

RE-ORDER LIST
················

CODE	DESCRIPTION
1234	PENS
2679	ERASERS
3456	RULERS
4567	WRITING PADS
6979	ENVELOPES
7050	CASH BOOKS

Table 11.2 Output from re-order program

A suitable program is listed in Table A20.

11.6 String functions

The string functions, briefly described in section 8.11, can be useful when manipulating data files. Their purpose is reiterated below with examples.

11.6.1 *LEN*

This function returns the length of a string. For example if string T\$ contained BASIC then,

$$10 \text{ LET } L = \text{LEN(T\$)}$$

would set $L = 5$.

11.6.2 *LEFT\$, RIGHT\$*

These functions return the leftmost or rightmost specified numbers of characters from a string, e.g.

$$10 \text{ LET } B\$ = \text{LEFT\$(T\$,2)}$$

returns the leftmost two characters from the string T$, i.e.
BS = BA, similarly,

$$10 \text{ LET } E\$ = RIGHT\$(T\$,3)$$

leaves E$ = SIC

11.6.3　*MID$*

This function returns a substring of n characters starting
with the ith character, i.e.

$$10 \text{ LET } C\$ = MID\$(T\$,2,3)$$

results in C$ = ASI　(n = 3, i = 2).

11.6.4　*CHR$*

This function returns the character corresponding to a
specified ASCII code (see Appendix C), i.e.

$$10 \text{ LET } A\$ = CHR\$(66)$$

The ASCII code for the letter B is 66, so the above statement
stores B in A$. Words can be built up by concatenation, i.e.

$$10 \text{ LET } A\$ = CHR\$(66) + CHR\$(69)$$

results in A$ = BE, where 69 is the ASCII code for E.
Note that as CHR$ returns the ASCII code, variables can
be set if required to the control characters (i.e. Return).

11.6.5　*ASC*

This function is the opposite of CHR$ in that it returns the
ASCII code number for a specified character, i.e.

$$10 \text{ LET } X = ASC(E)$$

results in X = 69.

Problem 3 – A data file search program

Write a program using string functions to search the stock data file produced in section 11.5 for any stock description containing a specified substring, i.e. PEN. An example of the output is shown in Table 11.3.

```
STOCK FILE SEARCH
.....................
ENTER SEARCH WORD ? PEN
PRESS PLAY ON TAPE # 1
OK
.............................................
CODE      DETAILS                    STOCK
.............................................
  1234    PENS                         15
  2340    PENCILS                      50
.............................................
11 RECORDS READ
2 RECORDS LISTED
```

Table 11.3   Output from search program

The program is listed in Table A21.

12 Applications

12.1 Series

A series consists of a number of terms, each term having a constant relationship to the next term. When devising computer programs for evaluating series, a procedure needs to be designed which allows the next term in the series to be calculated from the previous term.

For example, the exponential series may be evaluated as follows:

$$e^x = 1 + x + \frac{x^2}{2!} + \frac{x^3}{3!} + \ldots \to \infty$$

where $2! = 1 \times 2 \quad 3! = 1 \times 2 \times 3 \quad$ etc.

The steps in the repetitive process to calculate e^x to n terms are:

Step 1. (initialisation), set first term (T) to x, e^x to $1 + T$, and I to 2

Step 2. calculate next term by multiplying previous term by x/I, and add this new term to the old value of e^x

Step 3. repeat step 2 a further $n - 2$ times.

The BASIC routine to calculate e^x is shown in Table 12.1.

Problem 1 – Evaluation of cos x

Write a BASIC program for evaluating cos x, given that:

$$\cos x = 1 - \frac{x^2}{2!} + \frac{x^4}{4!} - \frac{x^6}{6!} + \ldots \to \infty$$

The program is listed in Table A22, and the value of cos 30° to 5 terms is given in Appendix B.

```
 20 PRINT "NO OF TERMS FOR E↑X";
 30 INPUT N
 40 PRINT "VALUE OF X";
 50 INPUT X
 60 LET T = X
 70 LET E = 1 + T
 80 FOR I = 2 TO N
 90 LET T = T*X/I
100 LET E = E + T
110 NEXT I
115 PRINT
120 PRINT "E↑";X;"=";E
125 PRINT "****************"
130 END
```

Table 12.1 Program to calculate e^x

12.2 Interactive running

The program given in Table 12.2 illustrates the use of the computer to process data which is entered at run time from

```
 10 PRINT "HEAT OF COMBUSTION"
 15 PRINT "------------------"
 20 PRINT "NAME OF SUBSTANCE";
 30 INPUT N$
 40 PRINT "ENTER S,W,T,R";
 50 INPUT S,W,T,R
 60 LET H = INT(W*4.2*T*R*0.001/S + 0.5)
 70 PRINT
 80 PRINT "RESULT FOR ";N$" = ";H;" KJ/MOL"
 85 PRINT "**********************************"
 90 PRINT
100 PRINT "ANY MORE DATA (Y = YES, N = NO)";
110 INPUT Y$
120 PRINT
130 IF Y$ = "Y" THEN 20
140 END
```

Table 12.2 'Heat of combustion' problem

the keyboard in response to messages output from the program. This method of working is applicable to, say, a class of students where each group is carrying out similar experiments. The results of the experiments are prepared for input to the computer program, and the program is used to output the final answer for each group. Similarly, a scientist

```
HEAT OF COMBUSTION
--------------------
NAME OF SUBSTANCE? ETHANOL
ENTER S,W,T,R? .36,100,23.5,46

RESULT FOR ETHANOL = 1261 KJ/MOL
***************************************

ANY MORE DATA (Y = YES, N = NO)? Y

NAME OF SUBSTANCE? METHANOL
ENTER S,W,T,R? .39,99,21.2,32

RESULT FOR METHANOL = 723 KJ/MOL
***************************************

ANY MORE DATA (Y = YES, N = NO)? Y

NAME OF SUBSTANCE? PROPANOL
ENTER S,W,T,R? .31,101,24.8,60

RESULT FOR PROPANOL = 2036 KJ/MOL
***************************************

ANY MORE DATA (Y = YES, N = NO)? N
```

Table 12.3   Output from Table 12.2 and data input

may repeat the same experiments for different substances and the series of results may then be processed by one computer program.

The output messages, replies (data input) and results are shown in Table 12.3. S is the mass of substance burnt and W the mass of water heated by the substance in grammes, T is the rise in temperature of the water in °C, and R is the relative molecular mass.

Problem 2 – Roots of quadratic equations

Write a program to calculate the values of the roots of any number of quadratic equations ($ax^2 + bx + c = 0$), given the coefficients a, b and c. If $b^2 - 4ac > 0$, output the message 'REAL ROOTS' and the two roots. If $b^2 - 4ac = 0$, output the message 'COINCIDENT ROOTS', and the value $= -b/2a$. If $b^2 - 4ac < 0$, output the message

$$3x^2 + 9x + 2 = 0$$
$$7x^2 - 5x + 3 = 0$$
$$x^2 - 8x + 16 = 0$$
$$2x^2 + 3x - 4 = 0$$
$$-3x^2 - 2x + 1 = 0$$
$$x^2 + 2x + 3 = 0$$
$$4x^2 + 4x + 1 = 0$$

Table 12.4 Quadratic equations

'COMPLEX ROOTS'. Allow for interactive entry of a, b and c during run time and stop the execution of the program by zeros being entered for a, b and c. The program is listed in Table A23, and the answers for the equations shown in Table 12.4 are given in Appendix B.

12.3 Tabulation of results and averaging

Measurements, intermediate calculations and final results of experiments may need to be tabulated so that a permanent record is available in an easily readable form. The final answer is often obtained by averaging the results of more than one experiment.

Problem 3 – Width of a slit

The collimator of a spectrometer was used to provide a parallel beam of light from a sodium flame. The beam of light was allowed to fall on a slit placed vertically at the centre of the table of the spectrometer. When appropriate adjustments had been made, parallel bands were seen on looking through the telescope. These were made as sharp as possible by adjusting the slit of the collimator. The cross-wires of the eyepiece of the telescope were set on corresponding minima on either side of the centre and the vernier readings were noted; this gave a value of 2A for each of the fringes 1 to 6.

The width of the slit W (cm) = $N\lambda/A$ where N is the fringe number, $\lambda = 5.893 \times 10^{-5}$ cm (wavelength of sodium light), and A is in radians.

Write a program to tabulate the measurements taken and values of A and W as shown in Table 12.5, and output the average value of the width of the slit. There are two pairs of

FRINGE NUMBER	VERNIER DEG	MIN	READINGS DEG	MIN	A MIN	WIDTH OF SLIT CM
1	41	26	41	20	3	6.75E-2
	221	25	221	19		
2	41	29	41	17		
	221	27	221	15		
3	41	33	41	15		
	221	31	221	13		
4	41	35	41	11		
	221	34	221	10		
5	41	39	41	9		
	221	38	221	8		
6	41	41	41	5		
	221	40	221	4		

Table 12.5 Tabulation of results for Problem 3

vernier readings for each fringe number. Values of 2A are found by subtracting the second vernier reading from the first vernier reading. The average value of A is then calculated for each fringe number. The program is listed in Table A24, and the average value of W is given in Appendix B.

12.4 Linear regression

Often straight line graphs may be obtained by manipulating the formula which defines the relationship between the variables. The equation of a straight line may be written as,

$$y = mx + c$$

where,

$x =$ the independent variable
$y =$ the dependent variable
$m =$ the slope of the line
$c =$ the intercept of the line on the y axis

A line of 'best fit' can be calculated for a series of data points from,

$$m = \frac{n\Sigma xy - \Sigma x\Sigma y}{n\Sigma x^2 - x^2}$$

and $c = \frac{\Sigma y - m\Sigma x}{n}$

where,
x and y are the co-ordinates of each data point and
n = number of data points.

There are many equivalent forms of the above expression; some are more suited to manual calculation than programming. A measure of how closely the data follows the calculated straight line is given by the coefficient of correlation (r). If the data lies on a perfectly straight line then r will be $+1$ (for positive slope) or -1 (for negative slope).

In the extreme case of no correlation whatsoever, i.e. the points are scattered randomly, r will equal zero. The acceptable level of correlation, i.e. value of r, for the number of readings involved can be found from statistical tables.

Again, the formulae for r can be presented in different ways. The expression given below is in a convenient form for programming when the slope is already evaluated.

$$r = \sqrt{\frac{m(\Sigma xy - \Sigma x \Sigma y/n)}{\Sigma y^2 - (\Sigma y)^2/n}}$$

It should be noted that m, c and r require similar preliminary calculations and that it is convenient to initially calculate and store,

$$\Sigma x, \ \Sigma y, \ \Sigma x^2, \ \Sigma y^2, \ \Sigma x \Sigma y$$

A program to perform linear regression and calculate r is given in Table 12.6.

Problem 4 – Young's modulus of the material of a bar

The bar was clamped horizontally at one end. A weight of mass M (kg) was attached to the other end, and was kept vibrating by an electro-magnet. The vibrating end of the bar was illuminated and was viewed through a slit in a rotating disc, using a telescope. The speed of the disc was gradually increased by adjusting the resistance, placed in series with the electric motor used to rotate the disc, until the bar appeared to be at rest when it was vibrating. A counting arrangement on the motor gave the number of rotations in a definite time.

It can be shown that the motion of the vibrating bar is simple harmonic with a period:

$$T = 2\pi \sqrt{\left(\frac{l^3(M + 33/140m)}{3Yi}\right)}$$

```
50   DIM X(20),Y(20)
60   PRINT "ENTER NO OF PAIRS OF READINGS ";
70   INPUT N
80   FOR I = 1 TO N
90   PRINT "ENTER X,Y PAIR ";
100  INPUT X(I),Y(I)
110  NEXT I
120  GOSUB 4000
130  STOP
4000 LET S1 = 0
4010 LET S2 = 0
4020 LET S3 = 0
4030 LET S4 = 0
4040 LET S5 = 0
4100 FOR I = 1 TO N
4110 LET S1 = S1 + X(I)
4120 LET S2 = S2 + Y(I)
4130 LET S3 = S3 + X(I)↑2
4140 LET S4 = S4 + Y(I)↑2
4150 LET S5 = S5 + X(I)*Y(I)
4160 NEXT I
4170 LET M = (N*S5 − S2*S1)/(N*S3 − S1↑2)
4180 LET C = (S2 − M*S1)/N
4190 LET R = (M*(S5 − S1*S2/N))/(S4 − S2↑2/N)
4192 PRINT
4194 PRINT " Y = (";M;" *X ) + ";C
4196 PRINT
4197 PRINT "COEFF. OF CORRELATION = ";SQR(R)
4198 RETURN
5000 END
```

Table 12.6 Linear regression routine

where i is the moment of inertia of cross-section
       Y is Young's modulus of the material of the bar
       l is the length of the bar in metres
       m is the mass in kg of the vibrating part of the bar
   For a bar of rectangular cross-section (breadth b and
depth d metres), $i = bd^3/12$.

Hence, $$\frac{3Ybd^3T^2}{48\,\pi^2 l^3} = M + 33/140m$$

T^2 (seconds) plotted for different values of M (kg) gives a straight line graph, and Y may be found using the slope of the graph as follows:

$$Y = \frac{1}{\text{slope of graph}} \cdot \frac{16\,\pi^2 l^3}{bd^3}$$

Write a program to output Young's modulus for a bar in Newtons/m². Use the linear regression routine given in

M (kg)	T (seconds)
.097	0.12
.147	0.139
.157	0.145
.177	0.15
.197	0.16

Table 12.7 Data for Problem 4

Table 12.6, to find the slope of the graph for the values of T and M given in Table 12.7. The dimensions of the bar are: b = 1.58 cm, d = 0.312 cm, l = 40 cm. The results are given in Appendix B.

Note: Remember to calculate T^2 for the linear regression 'Y' values; the 'X' values are those listed under M.

12.5 Simulation

12.5.1 *Background*

Simulation requires the writing of a program that models a situation. Changes are brought about in the model, either by the user or by inbuilt routines so that the behaviour of the model can be studied. From studying the behaviour of the model under varying circumstances it is hoped to gain a better understanding of the reality represented by the model.

Some models consist of specific relationships, e.g. a Balance Sheet. In such a case, if you make a change in one variable this leads to a specific revised Balance Sheet. You can, by this means, simulate the effect of changes in labour costs on the profits.

Many forms of simulation require the values of some of the variables to be sampled from a probable range of values. The probable range of values is usually expressed as a probability (or frequency) distribution. In these models, the outcomes and their interactions need to be studied over many simulations to obtain a representative picture of the model's behaviour.

A simple simulation model of this type is discussed below. As the basis of the variability is the sampling from a frequency distribution, the program has been written to make use of the two subroutines previously developed in Chapter 10, section 10.6. Note how the subroutine can be used several times by transferring values to and from the variables common to the subroutine.

12.5.2 *Simulation of combined units*

The problem is to simulate the breakdown pattern of a combined unit comprising a motor assembly and a gear assembly from the breakdown pattern of the individual assemblies.

The running time of a combined unit can be simulated by sampling in turn from the running time distributions of the motor unit and the gear unit. The shorter running time will be the running time of the combined unit. By simulating many such samples the MTBF (mean time between failure) for a combined unit can be obtained.

12.5.3 *Output required*

For a short simulation it is convenient to monitor the course of each pass through the program. Therefore, in this case, the output can be the sampled lives of the motor and gear assemblies, the life of the combined unit and the MTBF to date. For longer simulations this amount of detail would be time consuming to print. It could be incorporated for debugging purposes and then dropped, the final program only producing the ultimate MTBF.

However, a single final statement of the value of the MTBF is not as informative as a running output of the variable. The decision to terminate a simulation is often taken once the variable under inspection has settled down. These considerations, in this case, lead to the idea that there should be an option to continue the run if the fluctuation in the MTBF is not within the desired limits.

12.5.4 *Description of the program*

The BASIC listing of the main routine is shown in Table 12.8 and of the subroutines in Tables 10.12 and A18 (see Chapter 10).

The motor unit frequency distribution is input after control is transferred to the subroutine from line 40. The input is returned in array D and the contents copied to array M. This allows array D and hence the subroutine to be used again. This time the gear unit frequency distribution is input and on return to the main routine it is copied from array D to array G.

The next stage of the program initialises the variables T and K in readiness for the simulation. Variable T is the cumulative combined unit running time, and variable K is the starting (or continuation) value of the simulation count. K is initially set at one for the first run (line 100) and is revised in line 370 in case the FOR loop is to be continued.

The initial length of the simulation is input at line 130. Line 150 and 160 print the required heading. PRINT U$ produces a line of dashes and is used to highlight the headings (lines 145 and 170). Each line of calculated output is produced within the FOR loop from lines 180 to 350.

```
20  DIM M(10,2),G(10,2),D(10,2),X(10,2)
40  GOSUB 800
50  FOR I = 1 TO N
52  LET M(I,1) = D(I,1)
54  LET M(I,2) = D(I,2)
56  NEXT I
60  GOSUB 800
70  FOR I = 1 TO N
72  LET G(I,1) = D(I,1)
74  LET G(I,2) = D(I,2)
76  NEXT I
80  LET U$ ="- - - - - - - - - - - - - - - - - - - - - - - - - - - - - -"
90  LET T = 0
100 LET K = 1
115 PRINT
120 PRINT "INPUT LENGTH OF SIMULATION";
130 INPUT L
140 PRINT
145 PRINT U$
150 PRINT "SIM";TAB(6);"MOTOR";TAB(14);"GEAR";
160 PRINT TAB(22);"COMB.";TAB(30);"MTBF"
170 PRINT U$
180 FOR S = K TO L
200 FOR I = 1 TO 10
202 LET X(I,1) = M(I,1)
204 LET X(I,2) = M(I,2)
206 NEXT I
```

Table 12.8 (1)   Main routine for simulation program

To sample from the motor unit distribution (array M) it is copied to array X by lines 200–206. The subroutine starting at line 900 is entered and a sample from array X is returned as variable V. In line 220 this value is retained for future reference as variable U1. This procedure is then repeated for the gear unit, the sampled value being retained as U2. Lines

280–300 carry forward the lower of the two values as variable C (this is the running time of the combined unit). The cumulative running time is calculated in line 320 and the current average running time (the MTBF) is calculated

```
210  GOSUB 900
220  LET U1 = V
240  FOR I = 1 TO 10
242  LET X(I,1) = G(I,1)
244  LET X(I,2) = G(I,2)
246  NEXT I
250  GOSUB 900
260  LET U2 = V
280  LET C = U1
290  IF U2 > U1 THEN 320
300  LET C = U2
320  LET T = T + C
330  LET A = T/S
335  LET A = INT(10*A)/10
340  PRINT S;TAB(6);U1;TAB(14);U2;TAB(22);C;TAB(30);A
350  NEXT S
355  PRINT U$
370  LET K = L + 1
380  PRINT
390  PRINT "ENTER ADDITIONAL SIMULATIONS"
395  PRINT "REQUIRED, OR ZERO TO STOP";
400  INPUT L
405  IF L > 0 THEN 420
410  STOP
420  LET L = K + L − 1
430  GOTO 170
```

Table 12.8 (2)   Main routine for simulation program

in line 330 as A. Having completed a pass through the FOR loop, a line of output provides the current simulated values of U1, U2, C and A.

After simulating the stipulated number of times (i.e. L), the FOR loop is left. In anticipation of continuing, the value of K is reset in line 370. Lines 390–400 allow you to reset L, or, if you enter zero, the run stops.

To separate this interactive part of the run from the previously calculated output, PRINT U\$ is now used in line 355. If the run is to be continued, control is returned to line 170 to separate the subsequent output in a similar way. This means of trying to keep the output tidy is best appreciated by studying extracts from a run of this program as shown in Table 12.9.

INPUT LENGTH OF SIMULATION ? 10

SIM	MOTOR	GEAR	COMB.	MTBF
1	16	18	16	16
2	16	14	14	15
3	8	16	8	12.6
4	16	18	16	13.5
5	16	14	14	13.6
6	8	14	8	12.6
7	12	22	12	12.5
8	20	22	20	13.5
9	16	10	10	13.1
10	4	14	4	12.1

ENTER ADDITIONAL SIMULATIONS
REQUIRED, OR ZERO TO STOP ? 5

11	16	14	14	12.3
12	12	14	12	12.3
13	16	18	16	12.6
14	16	16	16	12.8
15	12	18	12	12.8

ENTER ADDITIONAL SIMULATIONS
REQUIRED, OR ZERO TO STOP ? 0

Table 12.9 Example of output from Table 12.8

Problem 5 – Combined units simulation

Use the simulation program (Table 12.8) to calculate the mean time between failure for a combined unit consisting of motor and gear units having the failure pattern shown in Table 12.10. Simulate 100 failures. The answer is given in Appendix B.

Motor Unit		Gear Unit	
Life (weeks)	Cum % Freq	Life (weeks)	Cum % Freq
4	20	10	10
8	40	12	15
12	50	14	40
16	90	16	60
20	100	18	75
		20	80
		22	100

Table 12.10   Failure pattern of units

12.6   Financial

Many financial calculations relate to the calculation of interest over a period of time. A common example involving repayment of interest (and capital) is a mortgage repayment. Once a mortgage has been obtained there is little you can do about the repayments required. A computer program, however, could be particularly useful in examining the effects of changing the variables to assist in choosing the most suitable mortgage.

12.6.1 *Mortgage calculations*

The repayments required on a mortgage can be calculated
from the following formula:

$$R = \frac{Pi(1 + i)^n}{(1 + i)^n - 1}$$

where,

P = Principal (the amount borrowed)
n = duration of mortgage
i = interest rate per annum
R = required annual repayment

Many organisations providing mortgages allow you to
repay monthly. The monthly repayments are usually $\frac{1}{12}$ of
the annual repayments because they are regarded as simply
advance payments of the annual premium. These monthly
advance payments do not themselves earn interest.

12.6.2 *Requirements of the program*

In examining alternative mortgage proposals you would
want to change P, n and/or i as required. As successive
changes were made it would be useful to be reminded as to
the current values of these three variables.

This program is the type likely to be used by someone such
as a broker in a working environment. As he is not likely
to have any programming knowledge the PRINT messages
need to be clear and the data entered in the most natural
way. Thus the variables to be revised are indicated by
entering I, P or N rather than entering a numeric alternative
such as 1, 2 or 3. Although the program is slightly more
complex as a result, this is regarded as a secondary
consideration.

The input to the program is straightforward; the interest
rate is entered as a percentage (i.e. 12.5 not .125) as this is
how it is commonly quoted.

12.6.3 *Description of the program*

A listing of the program is given in Table 12.11 and an example of the output in Table 12.12.

```
30  DEF FNM(X) = INT(X/.01 + .5)*.01
40  PRINT "ENTER INTEREST RATE AS A % ";
50  INPUT I
60  LET I = I/100
70  PRINT "ENTER SIZE OF MORTGAGE ";
80  INPUT P
90  PRINT "ENTER PERIOD OF LOAN (YRS) ";
100 INPUT N
120 LET R = (P*I*(1 + I)↑N)/(((1 + I)↑N) −1)
130 PRINT "MONTHLY REPAYMENTS = ";FNM(R/12)
140 PRINT
160 PRINT "ENTER I,P OR N TO REVISE"
165 PRINT "INTEREST,PRINCIPAL OR YEARS"
170 PRINT "EXISTING VALUES ARE"
175 PRINT I,P,N
180 PRINT "OR ENTER S TO STOP"
190 INPUT A$
200 IF A$ = "S" THEN 350
210 PRINT "ENTER REVISED VALUE ";
220 INPUT X
230 IF A$ = "I" THEN 290
240 IF A$ = "P" THEN 310
250 IF A$ = "N" THEN 330
260 PRINT "REVISION ERROR : ";A$" ENTERED"
270 PRINT
280 GOTO 160
290 LET I = X/100
300 GOTO 120
310 LET P = X
320 GOTO 120
330 LET N = X
340 GOTO 120
350 END
```

Table 12.11 Program for mortgage calculation

Line 30 defines the function FNM which rounds to two decimal places thereby representing monetary amounts to the nearest pence. Lines 40–100 request the starting values of I, P and N. The annual repayment is calculated in line 120 and printed as a monthly repayment in line 130. A blank line

```
ENTER INTEREST RATE AS A % ? 12.5
ENTER SIZE OF MORTAGE ? 10000
ENTER PERIOD OF LOAN (YRS) ? 25
MONTHLY REPAYMENTS = 109.95

ENTER I,P OR N TO REVISE
INTEREST,PRINCIPAL OR YEARS
EXISTING VALUES ARE
.125        10000        25
OR ENTER S TO STOP
? P
ENTER REVISED VALUE ? 8000
MONTHLY REPAYMENTS = 87.96

ENTER I,P OR N TO REVISE
INTEREST,PRINCIPAL OR YEARS
EXISTING VALUES ARE
.125        8000        25
OR ENTER S TO STOP
? S
```

Table 12.12   Example of output from Table 12.11

(line 140) is printed before looping and producing revised output.

Line 160 allows you to revise optionally the values of I, P or N and line 170 reminds you of the current values. The option you enter is identified by the program over lines 200–250. If an inappropriate character is entered this character 'falls through' these lines and the error message (line 260) is printed. Otherwise the revised value entered in line 220 is assigned accordingly over lines 290 to 330. The program then loops back to line 120 to recalculate R.

Problem 6 – Monthly repayments

Run the program shown in Table 12.11 using the following data:

Interest rate, 11%
Loan, £15,000
Period of loan, 20 years

Then revise the loan to £20,000. The two monthly repayments are given in Appendix B.

Appendix

Appendix A
Programs (Tables A1 to A24)

```
20  INPUT T1,T2,M
25  PRINT
30  LET N2 = (T2 + M)/60
35  REM ADD INTEGRAL PART OF N2 TO T1
40  LET N1 = T1 + INT(N2)
45  REM CALCULATE MINUTES
50  LET N2 = T2 + M −INT(N2)•60
60  PRINT "STARTING TIME =";T1;"HOURS";T2;"MINUTES"
70  PRINT "NUMBER OF MINUTES ADDED =";M
75  PRINT
80  PRINT "NEW TIME =";N1;"HOURS";N2;"MINUTES"
95  PRINT "* * * * * * * * * * * * * * * * * * * * * * * * * * * •"
100 END
```

Table A1 Hours and minutes

```
20  INPUT A,E,P,N,R
25  PRINT
30  LET T = ((A + E)∗N + P)/R
40  PRINT "LENGTH OF STAY (NIGHTS)          :";N
50  PRINT "ACCOMMODATION (PER NIGHT) $:";A
60  PRINT "EXPENSES (MEALS ETC.)        $:";E
65  PRINT "ALLOWANCE FOR PRESENTS       $:";P
70  PRINT "EXCHANGE RATE ($ TO THE £)    :";R
80  PRINT
90  PRINT "POUNDS STERLING REQUIRED   £:";T
95  PRINT "********************************"
100 END
```

Table A2 Number of £s required

```
20  INPUT N,F,P,S,D
25  PRINT
30  LET C = N*(F + P + 2*S*(100 − D)/100)/100
40  PRINT "NO OF DELEGATES      :";N
50  PRINT "COST OF FOLDERS      :";P;"P EACH"
60  PRINT "COST OF PAPER        :";P;"P PER PAD"
70  PRINT "COST OF PENS (LESS";D;"%):";S;"P EACH"
80  PRINT
90  PRINT "TOTAL COST OF STATIONERY = £";C
95  PRINT "*********************************"
100 END
```

Table A3   Cost of stationery

```
10  PRINT TAB(10);"TEST PROGRAM USING"
20  PRINT TAB(9);"CONDITIONAL STATEMENTS"
30  PRINT
35  PRINT
40  INPUT A,B,C
50  IF A = 0 THEN 200
60  IF A = B THEN 110
70  IF A > B THEN 130
80  IF C = 0 THEN 160
90  PRINT "(B − A)/C =";(B − A)/C;" WHEN A =";A;" B =";B;" C =";C
100 GOTO 30
110 PRINT "A = B =";A
120 GOTO 30
130 IF C = 0 THEN 180
140 PRINT "(A − B)/C =";(A − B)/C;" WHEN A =";A;" B =";B;" C =";C
150 GOTO 30
160 PRINT "B − A =";B − A;" WHEN A =";A;" B =";B;" C = 0"
170 GOTO 30
180 PRINT "A − B =";A − B;" WHEN A =";A;" B =";B;" C = 0"
190 GOTO 30
200 END
```

Table A4   Using conditional statements

```
20 PRINT "CALCULATIONS FOR DIFFERENT CODES"
21 PRINT
22 PRINT
30 PRINT "CODE    X    Y    CALC. VALUE"
32 PRINT "- - - -   - - -   - - -   - - - - - - - - - - -"
34 PRINT
40 REM N = NUMBER OF SETS OF DATA
50 INPUT N
60 FOR I = 1 TO N
70 INPUT C,X,Y
80 ON C GOTO 90,100,110,120,130
90 LET R = X + Y
95 GOTO 140
100 LET R = X — Y
105 GOTO 140
110 LET R = X•Y
115 GOTO 140
120 LET R = X/Y
125 GOTO 140
130 LET R = X↑Y
140 PRINT TAB(1);C;TAB(8);X;TAB(13);Y;TAB(21);R
150 NEXT I
160 END
```

Table A5   Using the ON . . . GOTO statement

```
61 PAGE
63 PRINT "ENTER PRINT OPTION H,N,L OR F";
64 INPUT P$
65 IF P$ = "F" THEN 380
66 IF P$ = "N" THEN 130
67 IF P$ = "L" THEN 291
```

Table A6   Print options (amendments to Table 2.1)

```
70  REM PRINT LETTER HEADING
71  PRINT "ENTER NO OF SHEETS & PRINT POSITION";
72  INPUT N1,P
73  FOR I = 1 TO N1
74  PAGE
75  PRINT
76  PRINT
80  PRINT TAB(P) ;A$
90  PRINT TAB(P) ;B$
100  PRINT TAB(P) ;C$
110  PRINT TAB(P) ;D$
112  NEXT I
115  GOTO 61
```

Table A7   Letter headings (amendments to Table 2.1)

```
120  REM PRINT NOTEBOOK LABEL
130  PRINT "ENTER NO OF LABELS & NAME LENGTH";
140  INPUT N2,L
150  PRINT "ENTER NO OF LABELS PER PAGE";
151  INPUT N3
152  FOR I = 1 TO N2/N3
153  PAGE
154  FOR J = 1 TO N3

200  PRINT TAB(7) ;"*                        *"
210  PRINT TAB(7) ;"*                        *"
220  LET J1 = INT((20—L)/2)
221  PRINT TAB(7) ;"*";
223  FOR I1 = 1 TO J1
224  PRINT " ";
225  NEXT I1
226  PRINT N$;
227  FOR I1 = 1 TO J1
228  PRINT " ";
229  NEXT I1
230  PRINT "*"
235  PRINT TAB(7) ;"*                        *"
240  PRINT TAB(7) ;"*                        *"

281  NEXT J
282  NEXT I
283  GOTO 61
```

Table A8   Notebook labels (amendments to Table 2.1)

```
290 REM PRINT ENVELOPE LABELS
291 PRINT "ENTER NO OF LABELS PER PAGE & TOTAL";
292 INPUT N5,N6
293 FOR I = 1 TO N6/N5
294 PAGE
295 FOR J = 1 TO N5/2

371 PRINT
372 PRINT
373 PRINT
374 NEXT J
375 NEXT I
376 GOTO 61
```

Table A9   Envelope labels (amendments to Table 2.1)


```
20 PRINT "SIDES OF TRIANGLE";
30 INPUT A,B,C
40 LET X = (A*A + C*C − B*B)/(2*A*C)
50 LET R = B/(2*SIN(ATN(SQR(1 − X*X)/X)))
60 PRINT
70 PRINT "RADIUS =";R;"M"
75 PRINT "******************"
80 END
```

Table A10   Radius of circumcircle

```
10 DEF FNR(X) = INT(X/0.1 + 0.5) 0.1
20 DEF FND(U) = ATN(1) •4/180
30 PRINT "SIDES OF TRIANGLE CM ANGLE AREA"
40 PRINT "    A    B    C    DEG SQ CM"
50 PRINT "- - - - - - - - - - - - - - - - - - - - - - - - - "
60 INPUT A,B,C,D1
70 IF A < 0 THEN 250
80 IF D1 >0 THEN 130
90 LET S = (A+ B + C)/2
100 LET R = FNR(SQR(S•(S — A)•(S — B)•(S—C)))
110 PRINT TAB(2) ;A;TAB(9) ;B ;TAB(16) ;C ;TAB(30) ;R
120 GOTO 60
130 LET D = D1 •FND(U)
140 IF A = 0 THEN 190
150 IF B = 0 THEN 220
160 LET R = FNR((A•B•SIN(D))/2)
170 PRINT TAB(2) ;A;TAB(9) ;B ;TAB(22) ;D1 ;TAB(30) ;R
180 GOTO 60
190 LET R = FNR((B•C•SIN(D))/2)
200 PRINT TAB(9) ;B ;TAB(16) ;C;TAB(22) ;D1 ;TAB(30) ;R
210 GOTO 60
220 LET R = FNR((A•C•SIN(D))/2)
230 PRINT TAB(2) ;A;TAB(16) ;C;TAB(22) ;D1 ;TAB(30) ;R
240 GOTO 60
250 END
```

Table A11   Areas of triangles

```
10 DATA  CUBOID,CYLINDER,"HEXAGONAL  BAR"
20 DEF FNR(A) = INT(A/F + 0.5)*F
30 DEF FNP(U) = ATN(1)*4
40 PRINT "ENTER CODE AND F";
50 INPUT C,F
60 IF C = 0 THEN 250
70 PRINT "ENTER TWO DIMENSIONS    ";
75 INPUT D1,D2
80 PRINT "ENTER HEIGHT            ";
85 INPUT H
90 PRINT
100 ON C GOTO 110,130,150
110 LET A = D1*D2
120 GOTO 160
130 LET A = FNP(U)*D1*D1
140 GOTO 160
150 LET A = SQR(27)/2*D1*D1
160 FOR I = 1 TO C
170 READ N$
180 NEXT I
190 PRINT "VOL OF ";N$;" =";FNR(A*H);
195 PRINT " CUBIC CM"
200 PRINT "*********************";
205 PRINT "*****************"
210 PRINT
220 PRINT
230 RESTORE
240 GOTO 40
250 END
```

Table A12   Volumes of solids

```
20  INPUT N
30  DIM A(20),B(20)
40  FOR I = 1 TO N
50  READ A(I)
60  NEXT I
70  FOR I = 1 TO N STEP 5
80  LET K = 1
90  FOR J = I TO I + 4
100 LET B(J) = A(N + 1 − J)
110 PRINT TAB(6*K) ;B(J);
120 LET K = K + 1
130 NEXT J
140 PRINT
150 NEXT I
160 DATA 1,2,3,4,5,6,7,8,9,10,11,12,13
170 DATA 14,15,16,17,18,19,20
180 END
```

Table A13   Copying an array

```
 20 DIM A(5,5)
 30 INPUT M
 40 IF M = 0 THEN 260
 50 LET D = 0
 60 FOR I = 1 TO M
 70 FOR J = 1 TO M
 80 READ A(I,J)
 90 PRINT A(I,J) ;
100 NEXT J
110 PRINT
120 LET D = D + A(I,I) + A(I,M + 1 − I)
130 NEXT I
140 PRINT
150 IF M/2 = INT(M/2) THEN 180
160 LET N = INT(M/2) + 1
170 LET D = D − A(N,N)
180 PRINT "SUM OF ELEMENTS ON DIAGS =";D
190 PRINT
200 PRINT
210 RESTORE
220 GOTO 30
230 DATA 10,11,12,13,14,15,16,17,18,19
240 DATA 20,21,22,23,24,25,26,27,28,29
250 DATA 30,31,32,33,34
260 END
```

Table A14 Sum of elements

```
20 INPUT N
30 DIM A(14)
40 FOR I = 1 TO N
50 READ A(I)
60 PRINT A(I);
70 NEXT I
80 PRINT
90 FOR I = 1 TO N −1
100 LET E = 0
110 FOR J = 1 TO N − I
120 IF A(J) < = A(J + 1) THEN 170
130 LET S = A(J)
140 LET A(J) = A(J + 1)
150 LET A(J + 1) = S
160 LET E = 1
170 NEXT J
180 IF E = 0 THEN 260
200 FOR K = 1 TO N
210 PRINT A(K);
220 NEXT K
230 PRINT
240 NEXT I
250 DATA 15,12,3,20,22,22,9,4,23,2,0,−25,17,18
260 END
```

Table A15 Sorting a list of numbers

```
20 DIM V(100)
30 PRINT "ENTER NO OF YEARS"
40 INPUT N
50 PRINT
60 FOR I = 1 TO N
70 PRINT "% PASTURELAND, YR ";I
80 INPUT V(I)
90 NEXT I
100 PRINT
110 GOSUB 1010
120 STOP
```

Table A16 Plot of percentage pastureland

```
20  DIM V(100),X(15),F(15)
30  PRINT "ENTER NO OF PARISHES";
40  INPUT N
50  PRINT
60  FOR I = 1 TO N
70  PRINT "% PASTURELAND, PARISH ";I;
80  INPUT V(I)
90  NEXT I
100 PRINT
110 GOSUB 2000
120 GOSUB 3000
130 GOSUB 4000
140 STOP
```

Table A17   Pastureland histogram

```
800 PRINT
810 PRINT "NO OF ROWS IN FREQ DIST. ";
820 INPUT N
830 IF N < 11 THEN 850
840 PRINT "NOT MORE THAN 10, TRY AGAIN"
845 GOTO 800
850 PRINT
860 PRINT "INPUT X & CUM FREQ "
870 FOR I = 1 TO N
880 INPUT D(I,1),D(I,2)
890 NEXT I
899 RETURN
```

Table A18   Input subroutine

```
30 OPEN 1,1,1,"STK-DATA"
210 INPUT K,D$,S,C,R
215 PRINT#1,K
216 PRINT#1,D$
217 PRINT#1,S
218 PRINT#1,C
219 PRINT#1,R
230 IF K = 9999 THEN 250
240 GOTO 210
250 CLOSE 1
600 END
```

Table A19   Stock data file creation

```
30 OPEN 1
40 PRINT "RE-ORDER LIST"
45 PRINT "- - - - - - - - - - - - - -"
50 PRINT
60 PRINT "CODE","DESCRIPTION"
65 PRINT "- - - -","- - - - - - - - - - -"
70 PRINT
80 INPUT#1,K,D$,S,C,R
90 IF K = 9999 THEN 130
100 IF S > R THEN 80
110 PRINT K,D$
120 GOTO 80
130 CLOSE 1
140 END
```

Table A20   Re-order list

```
2 PRINT "STOCK FILE SEARCH"
4 PRINT "- - - - - - - - - - - - - - - - -"
5 PRINT
6 PRINT "ENTER SEARCH WORD ";
10 INPUT X$
15 L = LEN(X$)
20 OPEN 1
22 LET E = 0
24 LET F = 0
25 LET U$ = "- - - - - - - - - - - - - - - - - - - - - - - - - - - - - -"
27 PRINT U$
28 PRINT "CODE","DETAILS",,"STOCK"
29 PRINT U$
30 INPUT # 1,K,D$,S,C,R
35 LET E = E + 1
40 LET W = LEN(D$) − L + 1
50 IF K = 9999 THEN 800
60 FOR I = 1TO W
70 LET Z$ = MID$(D$,I,L)
80 IF Z$ = X$ THEN 100
90 NEXT I
92 GOTO 30
100 LET F = F + 1
110 PRINT K;TAB(10) ;D$;TAB(30) ;S
140 GOTO 30
800 CLOSE 1
801 PRINT U$
805 PRINT E;"RECORDS READ"
810 PRINT F;"RECORDS LISTED"
900 END
```

Table A21 Stock file search

```
20  PRINT "NO OF TERMS FOR COS X";
30  INPUT N
40  PRINT "VALUE OF X (DEGREES)";
50  INPUT X1
60  LET X = (X1*ATN(1)*4/180)↑2
70  LET T = 1
80  LET C = 1
90  FOR I = 2 TO N*2 STEP 2
100 LET T = (−1)*T*X/((I−1)*I)
105 LET C = C + T
110 NEXT I
115 PRINT
120 PRINT "COS";X1;"=";C
125 PRINT "****************"
130 END
```

Table A22 Cos X

```
10  DEF FNR(A) = INT(A/0.01 + 0.5)*0.01
20  PRINT "ROOTS OF QUADRATIC EQUATIONS"
30  PRINT "- - - - - - - - - - - - - - - - - - - - - - - - - -"
40  PRINT "ENTER A,B,C (ZEROS TO STOP)";
60  INPUT A,B,C
70  IF A = 0 THEN 210
80  LET D = B*B − 4*A*C
90  IF D < 0 THEN 150
100 IF D = 0 THEN 170
110 LET D = SQR(D)
120 PRINT "REAL ROOTS :      ";FNR((−B+D)/(2*A));
130 PRINT "    AND     ";FNR((−B−D)/(2*A))
140 GOTO 180
150 PRINT "COMPLEX ROOTS"
160 GOTO 180
170 PRINT "COINCIDENT ROOTS :     ";FNR(−B/(2*A))
180 PRINT "* * * * * * * * * * * * * * * * * * * * * * * * * *"
190 PRINT
200 GOTO 40
210 END
```

Table A23 Roots of quadratic equations

```
10 PRINT "WIDTH OF A SLIT"
15 PRINT "***************"
20 PRINT "ENTER WAVELENGTH";
30 INPUT L
40 PRINT
50 PRINT "ENTER NO OF FRINGES";
60 INPUT N
70 PRINT "ENTER TWO SETS OF VERNIER READINGS"
80 PRINT "FOR EACH FRINGE IN DEG & MIN"
90 FOR I = 1 TO N
100 FOR J = 1 TO 2
110 INPUT P(I,J),Q(I,J),R(I,J),S(I,J)
120 LET B(J) = P(I,J)*60 + Q(I,J) — R(I,J)*60 — S(I,J)
130 NEXT J
140 LET A(I) = (B(1) + B(2))/4
150 LET W(I) = I*L*60*180/(A(I)*ATN(1)*4)
160 NEXT I
170 PRINT
180 PRINT "FRINGE   VERNIER READINGS  A   WIDTH OF"
190 PRINT "NUMBER DEG MIN  DEG MIN MIN  SLIT  CM"
200 PRINT "- - - - - - - - - - - - - - - - - - - - - - - - - -"
210 PRINT
220 FOR I = 1 TO N
230 LET W(I) = INT(W(I)/0.0001 + 0.5)*0.0001
240 PRINT TAB(8) ;P(I,1) ;TAB(13) ;Q(I,1) ;
250 PRINT TAB(17) ;R(I,1) ;TAB(22) ;S(I,1)
260 PRINT TAB(2) ;I ;TAB(27) ;A(I) ;TAB(32) ;W(I)
270 PRINT TAB(8) ;P(I,2) ;TAB(13) ;Q(I,2) ;
280 PRINT TAB(17) ;R(I,2) ;TAB(22) ;S(I,2)
290 PRINT "- - - - - - - - - - - - - - - - - - - - - - - - - -"
300 PRINT
310 LET W = W + W(I)
320 NEXT I
330 PRINT
340 LET W = INT(W/N/0.0001 + 0.5)*0.0001
350 PRINT "WIDTH OF SLIT =";W;"CM"
360 PRINT "**************************"
370 END
```

Table A24   Width of a slit

Appendix B
Answers to Problems

Chapter 7

1 CALCULATIONS FOR DIFFERENT CODES

CODE	X	Y	CALC. VALUE
3	51	4	204
1	25	13	38
2	8	34	−26
5	4	3	64
4	62	5	12.4

Chapter 8

1 RADIUS = 443.334 M

2 SIDES OF TRIANGLE CM

A	B	C	ANGLE DEG	AREA SQ. CM
17.2	9.8	14.1		69.1
	74	98	125.4	2955.7
292		405	30.5	30010.7
10.3	15.6		69	75

3 VOLUME OF CYLINDER = 111.33 CUBIC CM

VOLUME OF HEXAGONAL BAR = 103118 CUBIC CM

VOLUME OF CUBOID = 155.8 CUBIC CM

Chapter 12

1 Cos 30° = 0.866025   (to five terms)

2 REAL ROOTS :   −.24   AND   −2.76
   COMPLEX ROOTS
   COINCIDENT ROOTS :   4
   REAL ROOTS :   .85   AND   −2.35
   REAL ROOTS :   −1   AND   .33
   COMPLEX ROOTS
   COINCIDENT ROOTS :   −.5

3 WIDTH OF SLIT = 6.75E-2 CM

4 Slope = 0.1096
   Coefficient of correlation = 0.9953
   Young's modulus = 1.92×10^{11} Nm^{-2}

5 The answer will vary slightly depending upon the selection of random numbers but should be close to 11.1 weeks.

6 Monthly repayments = 156.97 and 209.29, respectively.

Appendix C
ASCII Code (64 Character Set)

Character	Binary code	Character	Binary code
space	0100000	@	1000000
!	0100001	A	1000001
"	0100010	B	1000010
#	0100011	C	1000011
$	0100100	D	1000100
%	0100101	E	1000101
&	0100110	F	1000110
'	0100111	G	1000111
(	0101000	H	1001000
)	0101001	I	1001001
*	0101010	J	1001010
+	0101011	K	1001011
,	0101100	L	1001100
-	0101101	M	1001101
.	0101110	N	1001110
/	0101111	O	1001111
0	0110000	P	1010000
1	0110001	Q	1010001
2	0110010	R	1010010
3	0110011	S	1010011
4	0110100	T	1010100
5	0110101	U	1010101
6	0110110	V	1010110
7	0110111	W	1010111
8	0111000	X	1011000
9	0111001	Y	1011001
:	0111010	Z	1011010
;	0111011	[	1011011
<	0111100	\	1011100
=	0111101	]	1011101
>	0111110	↑	1011110
?	0111111	←	1011111

Index

Index

THE POCKET CALCULATOR

L. R. CARTER and E. HUZAN

A practical handbook to help you become familiar with the techniques of using a pocket calculator.

This is a book for both the beginner and the specialist which examines calculator applications from the basic functions to the wider range of problems in mathematical, scientific, financial and statistical matters. The techniques discussed are fully illustrated with examples and exercises at varying levels of difficulty.

E. Huzan is principal lecturer in Computing and L. R. Carter is principal lecturer in Management Science at Slough College of Higher Education.

TEACH YOURSELF BOOKS

COMPUTER PROGRAMMING FORTRAN

A. S. RADFORD

A modern digital computer is capable of performing over one million operations a second, each of which it has to be instructed to perform. The form in which instructions are given to the computer is called a program and this must be written in a code or language intelligible to the computer.

This book provides a basic course in Fortran, a computer language widely adopted for scientific and general purpose commercial use. It begins with an outline of the development of the digital computer and computer languages and by describing the technique of flow charts – the means of establishing the sequence of events to be performed by the computer. The remainder of the book is concerned with explaining, analysing and teaching the Fortran language, covering a wide variety of programs and operations. Exercises to develop the programmer's proficiency in Fortran are incorporated in the text, which has been realistically geared to the needs of the self-educator as well as to those of the computer science student.

TEACH YOURSELF BOOKS

COMPUTER-BASED SYSTEMS

JOHN RACE

A computer-based system is an organisation of *people*, with individual responsibilities, who use a computer to achieve a defined set of objectives. John Race presents an overall view of these systems, how they are designed and implemented, and what their consequences can be. He emphasises that a computer-based system will succeed only if the people involved work harmoniously with the computer using their own speciality.

Throughout, the emphasis is on the effect of computers in both businesses and daily life. Background information on techniques, equipment and programs is followed by a discussion of computer applications with particular emphasis on their speed of response (e.g. the use of computers in route planning, stock control, cheque clearing, reservation systems, etc.). The ethical questions raised by the use of computers are also discussed, together with possible future trends.

This is a book for those considering a career in computers, students of computer science who wish to give their studies a broader context, and anyone who wishes to know more about the machines which affect so many aspects of modern life.

John Race is a senior lecturer in the department of Computer Science at Brunel University.

TEACH YOURSELF BOOKS